Crappie

Crappie
A Fish for All Seasons

Dan D. Gapen, Sr.

ISBN: 0-932985-02-5
ISBN-13: 978-0-932985-02-6

First Edition: September 1974
Reprinted: January 1986
Reprinted: May 2011

Published by
Whitewater Publishing Co.
17810 87th Street
Becker, Minnesota, USA 55308

Prepress by North Star Press of St. Cloud, Inc.

Printed by Sentinel Printing, St. Cloud, Minnesota, USA

. . . Dedication . . .
To
"The Children"

for it is they who will reap our true intention . . .
it is they who will see fishing live or die . . .
they who will suffer for a destruction we may cause . . .

Let this book on the basic panfish fishing begin a new attitude towards both the people and the fish they pursue.

Let not the "lordly" bass hunter race by the silent crappie angler in a roar of self-importance . . . and act which has left many a crappie seeker nearly sunk and fishless.

Let all anglers respect rights of others and in so doing begin to preserve the world we call "Fishing."

It all begins with the children . . . children of all ages and a fish with silver sides.

. . . and to Old Ben Snurd, my "panfish mentor."

Ol' Ben and the young man he taught.

Acknowledgements

In our world of Crappie, this fish for all seasons, there are countless "tens of thousands" who weave the fabric which creates this sport where kids of all ages area seen to romp. It is all of them to which I owe my gratitutde. Their smiles, laughter, pride, and knowledge can be seen and read within the covers of this book. There are just to many to try to thank individually, but rest assured it was thoughts of them that brought this book to print. For that, I am eternally grateful.

A special thanks must go to Ol' Ben Snurd, lately departed to a world where crappie grow as big as salmon, for it was he who first guided this young man to the world of silversides. It was he who caused a northern lad to look twice and begin a lifelong appreciation of the fish called "crappie." It was he who brought adventure and mystery into crappie fishing. Before, only third-clase status had been placed upon this fish. Today, he ranks high on the list for this writer.

The "Crappie" truly a fish for kids of all ages.

Dan D. Gapen, Sr., author

Contents

Introduction 1

1   Crappie Cousins 7

2   Cold Weather Crappie 14

3   Crappie Behavior 19

4   The Complete Crappie Angler 24

5   The Insect Feeder 33

6   The Welcome Invasion 38

7   Special Spring Spots 49

8   A Crappie Cousin 60

9   Summer – Hot Fishing in Cool Places 67

10   "Brushing Up" on Crappie 75

11   Fly Fishing for Crappie 78

12   Lake Okachobee: A Panfish Paradise 87

13   Ol' Goggle-eyes & Distant Cousin Mojarra 92

14   Reservoirs . . . Angling Utopias 99

15   Rivers and Streams . . . Horizons Lost 107

16   How to . . . River Crappie 114

17   Where Crappie Is King 125

18   It's All About Panfish and Farm Ponds 138

19   Crappie Cookout 143

20   Fall and Winter – The Neglected Seasons 153

21   The Must-Have Panfish Lure 158

22   Crappie on Ice 162

23   All Season Panfishing: Summer & Winter 168

About the Author

For each person there is a moment in time which sees life stop . . . hold . . . hold . . . and then pass on. So it was for Dan D. Gapen, Sr., during those early years when the wilderness of Northern Ontario was home. It was here, in a world of drifting water, rushing rapids, gentle back-waters, and giant fish that such a hold in time molded inner fabric strength. The memories and their lessons are etched deep within this man.

Youthful years were spent in an outdoor world of new birth, creation, wilderness, serenity, and full meaning. Full meaning for a man such as Dan. D. Gapen, Sr. A man whose very heart is held fast to the natural environment that surrounds all of us. An environment to which Gapen will always return, for it is the culmination of this man's very being. It is here, and only here, that he feels freedom and separation from those who would destroy man's instinct to live a nat-ural way. Fishing is but one of these inner needs.

So, it is that Gapen, a caring naturalist remains on quote, that fishing remain a sport from which man derive a zest for life and hap-piness within. And, that those who need to compete not dominate the sport in such a manner that the fun is gone. Competitive fishing will, in the long run, destroy the sport.

Born April 9, 1932, on the shores of North America's giant Lake Superior, Dan D. Gapen, Sr., is considered the nation's top anglers. To most, Gapen is considered the country's number one riverman.

Within the covers of this revised edition of *Crappie, A Fish for All Seasons*, Gapen has passed along his knowledge, as well as the se-crets of others, on crappie fishing, its how-to's, where-to's, and whys. It is Dan's wish that once having read the pages within, you will go forth and enhance your stringer weight next time out.

Though he grew up outwitting huge northern pike, splashing brook trout, giant pot-bellied lakers and overweight walleye, Dan D. Gapen, Sr., would be the first to admit his eagerness to halt such pur-suits were a school of fat two-pound crappie to swim by.

A Knowing Friend

Introduction

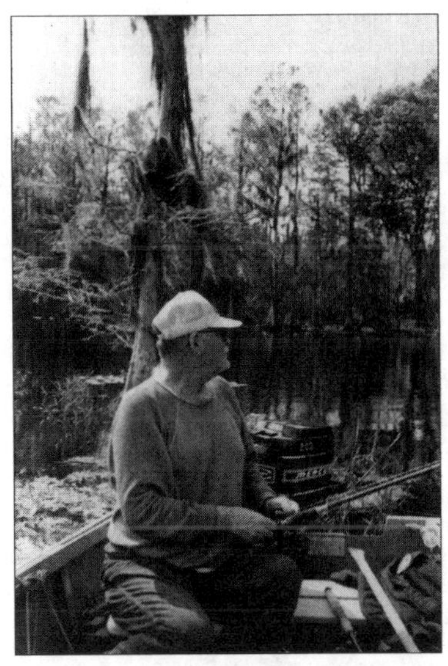
Ben Snurd

Memories . . . of those golden years as a youth in the Canadian wilderness and those crimson-bellied brook trout and northern pike as long as a canoe paddle . . .

Years later, of those battling bucket mouth bass in the Florida Everglades and their tireless leaps for freedom . . .

Of those granddaddy catfish in Kentucky's quiet woodland streams.

THESE ARE THE MOMENTS I remember as I relax in my woodland retreat. Memories flow and ebb like waves lapping endlessly on a rocky shore. "Bobber" Anne is in the kitchen preparing a dinner of fish and wild morels. My yellow lab Thumper is snuggled against the warm bricks of the fireplace.

Now, my mind drifts back to those not-so-pleasant outings. Those bright, sunny days when the walleye refuse to bite . . . when the *hog* largemouth bass sulked in watery lairs . . . when those capricious catfish would only *mouth* the bait then spit it out as if in disgust.

How many times has it happened? Angling for other fish proved fruitless, and so we would turn to *Ol' Silversides*, and before long, our stringers strained under the weight of slab crappies. Those were the days when the *Crappie Was King.*

My fishing memories are many. But treasured most of all are those fishing trips when all appeared hopeless, and then crappie came to the rescue.

I can remember one such outing with fond amusement. My partner was a snuff-chewing, bearded Alabamian by the name of Ben Snurd (his name alone should conjure up an impression of how he looked).

Old Ben and I were fishing crappie in northern Alabama using a technique known as *stump knocking*. I can't recall the name of the lake, but I do remember it as being a brackish swamp—a dark foreboding place like something right out of a Dracula movie.

Our adventures began amid a dense early morning mist punctuated by the eerie sounds of marsh birds and the creaking of ancient oar locks.

Old Ben weaved the flat-bottom boat between protruding cypress trunks and finally tied up to one of them. The ageless and battered stump appeared to have been burned off five feet above the water's surface. Of course, I didn't dare ask what caused a forest fire in the middle of a swamp. But, I remember thinking if it ever could happen, it *would* certainly happen here!

Ben's next move created even more questions in my already bewildered brain. He dragged out a long cane pile from somewhere beneath the boat seats and set about beating the rod rhythmically against several nearby stumps.

After three or four minutes of stump beating, he put the cane pole to its proper use. A ten-foot black line with an eighth-ounce white hair jig was tied to the pole. Sinkers and bobbers were ignored.

Ben lowered the white jig down through the center of the rotted stump, nothing happened. Next he tried the near side of the scarred trunk, still nothing. Then he tried the far side, christened the new spot with a spat of tobacco and promptly hoisted a glistening silver jewel from the dark water.

Three more times the technique was repeated while I stood silent with mouth agape. And three more times in quick succession Ben hefted a big white crappie over the gunwale. Amazingly, the stump beating hadn't frightened the fish away. Instead, it seemed to have lured the fish even closer to the gnarled old stumps so that one almost had to bounce the lure down the side of the trunk (or drop it through the middle) to get a strike.

In the days to come, I fished several other lakes with Ben Snurd, and each venture was a successful repeat performance. We caught crappie by the bushel-basketful, in addition to bluegill and bass. Naturally, Ben scoffed at the idea of keeping bass—crappie was his game.

I have not seen Ben since those wonderful days in Alabama some fifty-five years ago. Nor have I tried his stump-knocking technique since. But I will never forget the man—his grizzled, weathered face and gentle manner—nor his unique method of catching crappie, though I still ponder to this day why it worked so well. Maybe, as I lay by the fireplace with Thumper, some methods and techniques for catching fish should remain a mystery.

This book, like the first in our series, *Why fish Carp?*, is not designed to unravel all those wonderful fishing secrets that persist among the old sages. Instead, it is a simple, straightforward look at a very popular species of fish—how to find it, catch it and prepare it for the table.

It is estimated that our nation's vast legion of anglers spend more hours in pursuit of crappie than any other fish. But do crappie populations suffer from this enormous fishing pressure? Not at all. Each spring millions of crappie are snatched off their spawning beds and yet there are plenty around in the summer, fall, and winter to provide fishing fun.

Indeed, the crappie is a fish for all seasons—something for kids of all ages. Oh, sure, the walleye is a superb dinner fare. The northern pike is a brutal sparring partner. And, the smallmouth bass is a dazzling jumper. But what the crappie may lack as a fighter, he more than makes up for by his sheer abundance and the ease with which he can be caught.

Fancy equipment? Nope! My buddy "Bobber" Anne has her own precious memories of fishing during her younger years on a tiny creek on her family's turkey farm in central Minnesota.

Her equipment, a stout tree branch, a length of old string and a safety pin for a hook tipped with a juicy minnow found in a shallow pond. As you can see, it makes no difference whether you use a battered old cane pole or a $100 ultra-lite rig—either will catch crappie.

And so if you ask most anglers what they prefer to catch, they will probably pick the crappie. For the certainty of some type of fishing action is a whole lot better than the promised battle that never comes.

I am especially fond of the words of outdoor writer and avid angler Charles E. Most, who in an article for *Sport Fishing U.S.A.*, a book published by the U.S. Department of Interior, wrote . . . "Once while float-fishing Pennsylvania's Juniata River, I had a hard strike and saw a good-sized fish dash through a shallow area and into deeper water. I had apparently hooked a whopper smallmouth bass. After a hard fight that actually tired my arm I boated a good sized fallfish—a trash fish in most eastern streams.

"Here was a fish that struck savagely at an artificial lure and then gave me a tremendous battle. Was my disappointment because fallfish are not as good to eat as bass? Perhaps I just wanted a fish I could brag about.

"The soul-searching following these two experiences taught me not to be a fishing snob. I'm now convinced that any species of fish is a good catch—a prize worth the effort—and that any angler should go fishing when and where he can. Because, the finest fish I know just happens to be the one I'm currently trying to catch."

Enough said. Now come with us as we explore the world of the crappie. Let's learn the tried-and-true crappie fishing techniques used by anglers throughout the United States. It is a journey that we guarantee will be both fun and enlightening.

It is a journey filled with knowledge learned through seventy plus years in pursuit of Ol Silversides.

Along with crappie we will tell tales of his brothers, who may or may not be part of your fishing repertoire. Species such as perch, rock bass, bluegill, and all the brothers and sisters which host names such as stump knockers, red-ears, bream—all who hold a spot close to the all mighty crappie. All species, when challenged, can bring joy to those who angle for *"A Fish For All Seasons."*

~ Dan Gapen, Sr.

Chapter One
Crappie Cousins

Dan Gapen, Sr., and "Bobber" Ann show off a set of nice black crappie.

THE CRAPPIE, EVERYBODY'S FISHING favorite, is a member of the sunfish family (Centrarchidae), far and away the popular fish clan with American anglers.

The "first family" includes the freshwater basses, the true sunfishes, rock bass, Sacramento perch, flier, and two distinct crappie species—the black crappie (*Pomoxis nigromaculatus*) and the white crappie (*Promoxis annularis*).

Of course, the name game doesn't end here. The fishing favorite answers to more aliases than a "most-wanted" criminal. The crappie has been affectionately nicknamed Ol' Silversides, silvers, or slabbies by many anglers. But the U.S. Department of Interior in its book *Sport Fishing U.S.A.* listed fifty-five more! Which one of these monikers is your favorite?

Bachelor
Crapet
Pale Crappie
Ringed Crappie
Timber Crappie
Bachelor Perch
Bachelor Shad
Banklick
Banklick Bass
Barfish
Bigfin Bass
Bitterhead
Bride Perch
Bridge Perch
Calico Perch
Razorback
Roach
Sac-a-lait

Chinquapin
Chinquapin Perch
Dolly Varden
Goggle-Eye
Goggle-Eye Perch
Goldring
Grass Bass
John Demon
Lake Bass
Lake Erie Bass
Lamplighter
Millpond Bass
Newlight
Papermouth
Suckley Perch
Sun Perch
Tin Mouth
Tin Perch

Rockfish
Sago
Silver Bass
Silver Perch
Shad
Sand Perch
Speckled Bass
Speckled Perch
Speck
Spotted Perch
Spotted Trout
Straw Bass
Strawberry Bass
Strawberry Perch
Calico Bass
Calico Bream
Campbellite
White Perch

Little or small crappie are still a thrill to anglers.

Though anglers may differ widely in their pet names for the crappie, most would agree that it is one of our most beautiful sport fish with its silvery body, black markings, and its large delicately fanned fins.

Crappie are relatively fast-growing and short-lived, seldom surviving more than four to eight years. They usually attain an average length of two to three inches in their first year, five to eight inches at two years, seven to eleven inches by three years, and ten to fourteen inches at four years. Any further growth is usually slower.

The rate at which the crappie grows is related to the condition of the aquatic environment and such factors as food availability and competition for both food and space. In lakes with poor growth conditions, it is not unusual to find crappie weighing less than four ounces, but ready to die of old age.

Unless crappie can attain a length of ten inches in four years, they will not produce good fishing. Nationwide, the average crappie caught is three years old, about ten to twelve inches long and weighing about one pound.

Notable exceptions, however, can be found in the record books. The oldest known crappie was a thirteen-year-old fish taken from Croydon Reservoir in Iowa. It weighed three pounds, nine ounces.

The recognized world record black crappie weighed five pounds, measured nineteen and one-quarter inches in length and with an eighteen-and-five-eighths-inch girth. The lucky angler was Paul E Foust, who caught the fish in 1957 at South Carolina's Santee-Cooper Lake.

The year 1957 was indeed a very good year—the white crappie mark was also set that year. The trophy fish was taken from Enid Reservoir in Mississippi by Fred Bright of Memphis. It weighed five pounds, three ounces.

Sadly, the new black crappie record might have been set in 1969 but the lunker was eaten! Young Lettie Robertson of Louisiana caught a crappie that reportedly weighed six pounds even. The fish was weighed on state-inspected scales and had numerous affidavits to verify the catch.

Later, the fish was identified as a crappie in a photograph examined by a biologist for the Louisiana Wildlife and Fisheries Commission. But without positive identification as to whether it was a black or white crappie, it was ruled that the fish could not stand as an international record. Louisiana fisheries experts are still trying to unravel the mystery.

Black and white crappie, in addition to size, differ also in basic appearance and habitat preference.

Black Crappie

The black crappie prefers cool, clear lakes and large slow-moving rivers. It is a little more particular about its environment than the white crappie, which flourishes in warmer and siltier waters.

Generally, the black crappie has silvery-olive sides shading into olive-green on the back. Black spots or blotches are scattered irregularly over much of the fish. During spawning season, the splotches seem to grow in size to turn the entire fish a deep purple-black.

The easiest method of identifying the two species is to count dorsal spines. Usually, the black crappie has seven or eight dorsal spines, while the white crappie normally has six. This identification technique, however, is not foolproof as some white crappie have been found with seven spines.

The surest means of identification is to apply the following formula: the distance from the eye to the start of the dorsal fin is equal to the length of the base of the dorsal fin on the black crappie. On the white crappie the distance from the eye to the dorsal fin is greater than the length of the dorsal fin base.

Original range of the black crappie is southern Canada from Manitoba to the Upper St. Lawrence River in Québec, and southward through the Great Lakes. They are found in the Mississippi River drainage as far south as Texas and northern Florida. They also are distributed along the southern Atlantic Coast as far south as North Carolina.

Black crappie have been introduced widely into waters of the northeastern states and many of the western states, extending to the Pacific Ocean and as far north as British Columbia.

While the crappie has been widely accepted by most anglers, it is considered a "rough fish" in the state of Maine. Crappie were first introduced into Maine waters in 1921 when they were stocked into a tributary of Virginia Lake by an uniformed camp owner. Their population remains relatively static and locked in by natural barriers within Maine's Crooked River watershed.

Maine biologists consider the introduction of the black crappie as "unwise" because the fish compete with native smallmouth bass for food and space. In an article in *Maine Fish and Game Magazine*, a biologist wrote that introduction of crappie in lakes and ponds in Maine can have "serious detrimental effects on fish species already present. Every effort should be made to protect other water of Maine from this unwelcome guest."

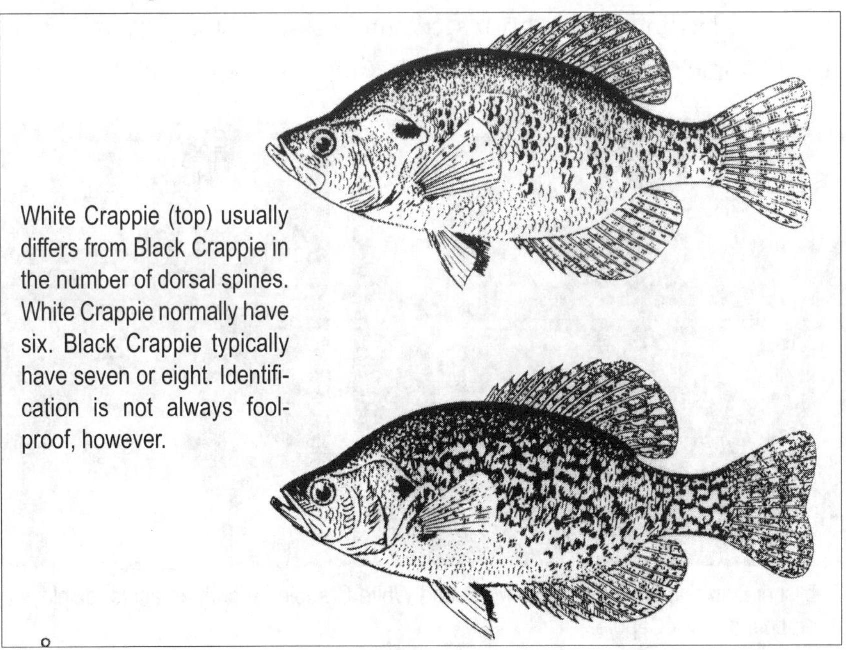

White Crappie (top) usually differs from Black Crappie in the number of dorsal spines. White Crappie normally have six. Black Crappie typically have seven or eight. Identification is not always foolproof, however.

White Crappie

White crappie, in addition to the usually different dorsal spine count, differ from their black cousins in that the white's black spots are not as dark and are arranged into seven to nine vertical bars extending down the sides of the fish from its dark-olive back.

The original distribution of white crappie was from Nebraska eastward to Lake Ontario and southward through the Ohio and Mississippi rivers watersheds to Texas and Alabama and northward to North Carolina. It too has been introduced in lakes and reservoirs in many other states. Some white crappie, for example, still survives in the San Diego, California, area where they were stocked in 1891.

Ranges of the crappie cousins overlap from state to state. Both species were introduced in Colorado in 1882, though white crappie today make up a greater proportion of the warm-water anglers' catch. Because of this great overlapping in territories the location of the catch should not be considered a safe guide to identification.

Both crappie species have similar aquatic menus. Crappie are carnivorous, feeding mostly on insects, mollusks, crustaceans, and small fish. Crappie have the most efficient feeding apparatus of all the sunfish

Publisher Dan Gapen (left) with a two-pound White Crappie. At right an angler displays a three-pound Black Cappie.

species. The gill-rakers are fine, numerous and long. They can strain from the water some of the smallest forms of animal life, although the most important food items are insects and minnows. In southern reservoirs, gizzard shad make up more than fifty percent of the crappie's diet, while in most other regions of the United States and particularly the northern states, insects play a greater part in their dining habits.

Crappie, perch, and white bass, surprisingly, all may prey on young walleye, northern pike, and largemouth bass. For this reason alone, stocking very young walleye and pike in panfish-dominated waters is often unsuccessful and a waste of taxpayer's money.

When crappie become too dominant in a lake, stunting can result. Stunted fish often are too small for eating, and anglers may have to fish long hours to catch a meal. When crappie are too abundant, the obvious corrective action is to drastically reduce their numbers—either by netting or chemicals—so fish will have enough food to grow and develop. Unfortunately, most fishermen are not ready to accept such a solution.

The general opinion remains that fish require only time and water to grow. Instead of permitting a major reduction of the population of stunted fish, additional stocking is demanded. This, of course, only makes matters worse.

Stunting, it should be emphasized, usually does not occur in a lake with a healthy balanced fish population with a suitable predator-prey ratio.

Blooming of berry trees is crappy time in the Ozarks.

Chapter Two
Cold Weather Crappie

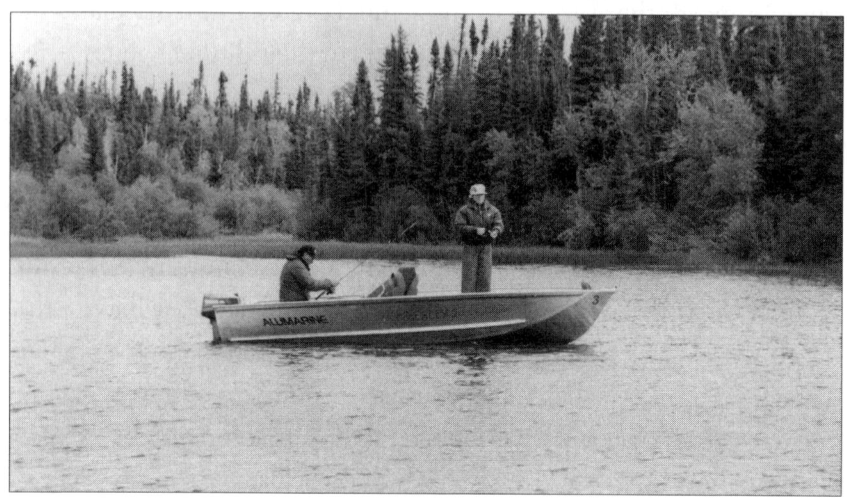

Having described what a crappie is in Chapter One, let me go on and tell a story about one of the greatest crappie holes in the north I know.

In the northwest arm of Lake of the Woods in Ontario, Canada, huge schools of black crappie gather in late September and early October. This migration of Ol' Silversides is triggered by a shift in weather as northwest winds blow hard and icy. Instead of seeking the shallows of spring where reproduction occurs, this run comes on with the need to find winter staging cover.

At the invitation of Tom Pearson of Camp Narrows Lodge, "Bobber" Anne and I accepted his tempting invite to fish the cold-weather crappie that crowded in for winter and lay only yards in front of this lodge's cabins. Once there, they'd hold their positioning in the deep channel waters throughout the winter.

Crappie, a fish of all seasons, is generally harvested by the angler in early spring when the time of spawn is on. With the fish staging in shallow water structure, the anglers easily find their prey. In waters no deeper than ten feet, the silver-sided fish can be sighted as it goes about the act of reproduction. In fall on the northwest arm of Lake of the Woods, crappie hold between thirty and forty feet. They station in such depth that ninety percent of them brought to the surface get the bends and resist any release technique that might save them. No amount of tactics such as "fizzing" or "deep-thrusting" work. Releasing the small ones only result in a puffed up stomach and a dying fish floating on surface.

There is one thing these floating panfish create—an influx of eagles that gather to feed on the bloated crappie carcasses.

Camp Narrows is a drive-to, boat-in resort. We were met at the landing at LaBelle's Birch Point Resort by Tom Pearson, and twenty minutes later were in our woodstove-warmed cabin. The weather was cold with a rain and sleet mix falling.

Our host, Tom, made mention that we should give it a go even though we arrived late in the day.

"Folks, we only have to go 250 yards off your cabin porch to find fish," Tom indicated out the window.

That wouldn't be too bad! Bundled up in winter gear, we headed out. Soon our graph showed a red blob of fish positioned at twenty-three feet over a depth of thirty-five feet.

Crappies—Lots of Them!

Tom would use an old tried-and-true setup. An one-eighth-ounce jighead tipped with a two-inch fathead minnow would be his offering.

Anne and I, true to our company's theme, hooked on an one-sixteenth-ounce Flicker and an one-sixteenth-ounce Freshwater Shrimp, both proven winners on crappie.

Tom struck fish first—a nice sixteen-inch fish which bounced to surface once it reached about five feet of depth. The bends did indeed occur. My Flicker got struck next, and an exact copy to Tom's came on board.

Before either of us could place our fish in the cooler, Anne had a seventeen-incher brought up. If this kept up we'd have our twenty-five-fish limit for each of us on board within the hour.

Next came a series of fourteen to fifteen inchers, all of which had to be kept because of the bloating effect created by the cold, deep water. Finally, when I boated an eleven incher, I attempted to release it, but the effort failed. No matter how deep I thrust the fish, it would instantly pop back up to surface because if the bloated air bladder.

"Dan, I have a way to cure that, but I'm not sure they live after the procedure is performed," commented Tom as he withdrew a needle-like device from his pocket.

Carefully Tom inserted the needle beneath the scales on the right side of the fish. Instantly, the bloated bladder deflated, and one the fish was released it swam straight down to join its buddies. "Fizzing" had been performed.

There is much controversy regarding this attempt at fish-saving. Some claim the fish dies anyway soon after being released. Others claim it's the best thing to do when you want to release them. I can never get an answer from the fish experts, backed with statistical proof if it works or not. But, on the dozen or so crappie on which we performed fizzing in the three days we fished at Camp Narrow it appeared to be the answer to save the small ones.

What exactly is fizzing? Fizzing is an operation performed by anglers to release fish which have been subjected to the bends after coming out of deep water. Most of the time cold deep waters create this condition. To fizz a fish, a sharp, fine, hollow needle is inserted into the fish's bloated air bladder to release pressure created when the fish is raised to surface too quickly.

Finally, with twenty-one fish in the cooler, we decided we'd had enough. The light rain had turned to snow, making fishing extremely uncomfortable. Furthermore, twenty-one fish was enough to clean. Tomorrow would be a better day.

Day two saw us out on the lake, three blocks from camp. Today, without the drizzle or snow, we'd attempt to film our show, *Fishing the World with The Ol' Man and "Bobber" Anne.*

As on the previous day, numerous red blobs of crappie schools appeared on the graph instantly as we reached thirty-five feet of depth. Today, the schools didn't seem to be as large but there were more of them. Our host insisted it was a good sign. Instead of the old trick, jig and minnow tip, Tom had elected to use one of our Flickers. He'd noted how well this number-one ice jig had done for Anne and me the day before and requested the use of an one-eighth-ounce size in silver, his theory being the bigger the offering the bigger the crappie.

Once again, as we all dropped our Flickers into the school below, we hit fish. It was three on at a time, time after time. Finally, with twelve fish in the cooler, Anne made mention that, "Shouldn't we be filming this action, Dan?" She was right! From that point on, one or the other of us took turns filming the catching. Rest assured, with this fast action, it didn't take long to film a thirty-minute TV show. This day ended as a heavy northwest wind blew us off the water at noon. Counting our catch back at the dock, we'd collected twenty-nine fifteen- to seventeen-inch crappie. The slabs they provided were as large as most walleye this region produced and just as good eating.

We didn't get back on the water until 5:30 that evening. The crappies were still there, but the cold front had blown their mouths shut. Only seven fish were taken that evening, all small ones at that.

Our last day saw winds switch to the west and air temperatures rise. We would once again take our limits.

I've fished Toledo Bend, Kentucky Lake, and many of the TVA reservoirs where crappie come big and easy, but this catch, minus the weather, may have been one of my top five crappie adventures. It was especially productive because the crappies were black crappie, and they come from ice cold northern waters. The flesh was extra firm and extremely delicious.

My suggestion to anglers is to look up Camp Narrows on the Internet and book a fall trip.

"Bobber" Anne shows off a cold-weather crappie enticed by a Flicker.

Chapter Three
Crappie Behavior

In spring, when the frogs begin their nightly chorus and the quail whistle their courtship calls, the crappie, too, respond to an inner urge as old as life itself.

When water temperatures climb into the sixty-degree range, crappie move from deep water into the shallows where they will go about the business of propagating their species.

Crappies are the earliest spawners of all species in the sunfish family. Ideal spawning temperatures vary from region to region. In Washington, for example, researchers have found crappie actively spawning when water temperatures approach fifty-five degrees. But in most waters, sixty-five to sixty-eight degrees is considered the ideal range.

Like other sunfishes, the crappie is a nest builder. The male prepares the nest by fanning out a circular area on the lake bottom in a water depth from three to eight feet. Some fish, however, may nest in water so shallow that their backs protrude above the surface.

The crappie is particular as to where it nests. The bottom must not be soft and muddy or silt would settle over the eggs, killing them before the tiny fish ever hatch. Instead, crappie look for bottom material of hard-packed sand, gravel, shell or marl (loosely packed clay and limestone). They also prefer areas where there are reeds, light aquatic growth, stickups, or scattered brush.

Once the nest is cleaned of debris and silt, the male then guides a female to the nest where her eggs are deposited and fertilized. As the eggs are released, their adhesive surfaces cause them to stick to weeds and brush in the nest. A half-pound female crappie will lay from 20,000 to 50,000 eggs, though the number varies from fish to fish and lake to lake. Biologists have taken as few as 3,000 eggs from an adult female and as many as 158,000!

After egg-laying and fertilization is completed, the male will then remain near the nest, zealously guarding and protecting the eggs from all adversaries.

The eggs begin to hatch within seven to fifteen days depending on water temperature. As soon as the young fry are hatched, the struggle for life begins. The first young crappies to perish are usually those eaten by the same male who had so fearlessly guarded them as eggs. Other fry will soon succumb to minnows or small game fish such as perch, sunfish, or other crappie.

Many anglers have been mystified by severe fluctuations in crappie populations in their favorite lakes. Too many predator fish, pollution, and overfishing are blamed. But population decreases are sometimes caused by the crappie themselves.

In a good year, when spawning and food conditions are ideal, crappie, with their tremendous reproductive potential, will produce an extremely large brood of young fish. This brood is known as the dominant year class.

In the years to come, the dominant brood devours its own young as well as that of other fish. This annual eradication continues until the original brood has decreased to the point that surviving members no longer can remove the yearly hatch. Once this point is reached, crappie populations begin to increase until the adults again become so abundant that they devour almost all their young.

During those periods of super-abundance, fishermen find little difficulty bringing home limits of catchable-size fish, but only a small percentage of the fish will fall into the "lunker" or two-pound category.

Slip bobbers such as Gapen Slip-N-Lock float along with a tiny one-thirty-second-ounce Freshwater Shrimp jig will find crappie no matter at what seasonal depth they stay.

During spring the spawning crappie are reasonably predictable and cooperative. But with warmer temperatures and the onset of balmy summer weather, their mood changes and they becomes unpredictable and elusive to many anglers.

After spawning, adult crappie school again in deeper water where they begin their summer wanderings for food. They may range far and wide during summer months in search of food and the right living conditions—primarily cool, well-oxygenated water.

In Tennessee Valley Authority reservoirs it was discovered during a series of studies that crappie moved an average of 5.4 miles. In comparison, smallmouth bass traveled only 1.2 miles, largemouth bass four miles, and walleye an average minimum distance of 11.6 miles.

In summer, crappie may be found in water varying anywhere from three to thirty feet. During the peak feeding periods—usually early morning or evening—they can be found in shallow weedy bays or around drop offs and off-shore brush piles where they prey on minnows. But during the heat of the day, crappie almost always seek the comfort of cool, shaded water.

Massive schools of crappie form at different layers of the lake—wherever the fish locate ideal water temperatures. These large schools spread out through the water laterally rather than vertically—a phenomenon especially characteristic of crappie in large reservoirs. In these large waters, temperatures vary considerably more from surface to lake bottom, compared to smaller bodies of water, where lake temperature is more uniform.

As the days grow hotter and the water continues to warm, crappie may head even deeper to find cooler water or they may seek out stream channels or any depressions in the lake bottom. Springs and small streams which bring cool water are other popular resting areas.

Summer will also find crappie moving into other shaded areas—under piers, bridges, boat docks, or at the base of old tree stumps. Many crappies are caught in ten to fifteen feet of water inside old trees which have been flooded.

With the coming of autumn, crappie may move into even deeper waters to gather around underwater structures such as old channels, rocky ledges or around deep weed beds. Though they will move up to find food and occasionally hang in shallower water, crappie will generally remain in these deeper waters until spring when they invade the shallows once again to reproduce.

Crappie may well be the fish which sees your child lauch into a lifetime of fishing.

Above: When weather cools, crappie will return to the shallow structures once used for spring spawning.

At left: A youthful author lifts a stringer of Kentucky Lake white crappie.

A stringer of small crappie kept will do little to lessen this fish's population.

Net-loads of crappie can be kept to satisfy the urge to eat fish.

# Chapter Four
The Complete Crappie Angler

While the crappie lacks the awesome power of the smallmouth bass and the ferocity of the northern pike, it is one of our most popular sport fish simply because of its abundant and the ease with which it is caught.

Thus, in selecting crappie tackle, the emphasis should not be on strong equipment or heavy line but on tackle that is light, well-balanced and easy to operate.

My fishing partner, "Bobber" Anne joyfully recalled her days as a youngster in the Melrose farm country of Central Minnesota. Memorable hours were spent by a small farm pond where she caught many crappies. Her fishing gear consisted of nothing more than a six-foot bent and twisted tree branch and a ten-foot length of yellow string.

She remembers with great satisfaction her first two-pound crappie, a muscular fish attired in its deep bluish-black spawning robe. She caught the lunker on a common safety pin and a small white grub.

Tip: I've found that line that takes on a twesting set can be stretched and reused numberous times. Take the end of your line, tie it to a tree or porch rail and walk off 100 feet or so. Next, by holding the line on the spool so it doesn't slip with drag movement, pull hard. With 100 feet out, you may experience as much as six feet of stretch. Repeat this hard pull several times until the line lays flat, with all the twist taken out. Now reel it back onto the spool. You have just saved yourself dollars, and the newly stretched line will act as if it was new. This tip will also clear up any new line you spool on and find it springs off the spool. If you doubt my simple little tip, do the following: If you doubt my simple little stretching trick, at least do the following: after every second or third fishing trip, strip off fifteen yards and throw it away. (But be careful it doesn't go overboard where it could ensnare or be ingested by waterfowl or other birds.) Remember monofilament line doesn't rot or weaken like other lines.

The versatile cane pole is popular with crappie fishermen everywhere.

Virtually any rod-and-reel combination, cane pole, or even a tree branch will provide enjoyable crappie fishing. But for the ultimate in panfishing, the ultra-light spinning combo, is well worth a small investment. An open-faced ultra-light reel along with a lightweight five- or six-foot rod makes even the half-pound crappie a game fighter. And a two-pounder will set the little rod to whipping like cane grass in a hurricane.

Any good quality four- or six-pound-test line is sufficient for ultra-light spinning. What is good quality line? It's almost any monofilament line sold in stores today. In fact, when anglers ask me about fishing line, my advice is, "It's not what line you purchase but how you take care of it that counts."

Whatever you do, don't be one of those anglers who changes line once a year, "whether it needs it or not!"

One other thing—monofilament generally doesn't knot or weaken unless left in the sun for extended periods of time.

The ultra-light rod and reel outfitted with monofilament line enables the angler to pinpoint the casts toward deadfalls, stumps, and small pockets in dense aquatic vegetation. To enhance casting accuracy, rig a small split-shot from four to eight inches above your bait. This added weight will also increase casting distance.

Another popular crappie combination is the cane or fiberglass pole in lengths of from sixteen to twenty-four feet. A favorite is the light weight and extremely durable telescoping pole in a sixteen-foot length.

You may want to use different length rods for different types of fishing. One that enables you to fish eight to ten feet from the boat is adequate. However, if fishing from shore, you may need a longer pole.

Under no circumstances should your line be longer than your pole, or you will be unable to control the line as you swing a crappie on board. Some anglers use twenty-foot poles, but with only five feet of line. If a fish is hooked, the angler brings the rod toward him, hand-over-hand until he reaches the last five feet of the pole, when he boats the fish.

Proper rigging for a cane or fiberglass pole is to tie on a nylon leader and a small split-shot about four inches from a #6 or #8 long-shanked, soft-wire hook. (The reason for the thin-wire hook will be discussed later.)

Most anglers use a small float with either a cane pole or rod and reel. There are a number of small casting bobbers on the market. My favorite is the Slip-n-Lock type, which creates a minimum of disturbance on the surface but is easily visible. Cane pole fishermen, however, generally prefer quill-type floats such as a pencil float.

There are many times when floats are not advisable. When crappie are biting light, even a faint resistance of the bobber may cause them to spit out the bait.

What is the best crappie bait? Are artificials more effective then natural baits—or vice versa? This has been the subject of considerable debate for over a century.

I remember a spring day many years ago when our family was fishing a small stream that emptied into a western Minnesota lake. We fished from a steep river bank. Below us a school of crappie was feeding ravenously. It was only a matter of ten minutes before we ran out of minnows. Fortunately, an old timer happened along and shared with us one of his favorite angling tricks. He provided us with small, white rubber bands which he knotted on our hooks. Shortly, with the aid of the rubber bands, we had filled a gunny sack with black crappie. Today I'd use a white one-and-one-half-inch Nasty Wacker, a lure that readily duplicates the old timer's rubber bands.

This incident may be stretching (pardon the pun) my point a bit, but usually crappie are not too finicky in their choice of baits. After speaking with hundreds of anglers throughout the county, the best all-around crappie rig seems to be a combination of both artificial and live bait—namely a colorful hair jig (called flies in some locales) combined with a small minnow does the trick.

The size of the jig may vary, but our favorite weights are one-eighth, one-sixteenth and one-thirtysecond ounce. All three sizes can be easily cast with lightweight or standard spinning equipment, or with a fly rod if need be. The favorite jig colors vary considerably among anglers, but white, yellow, chartreuse, red, and black seem most popular with blue or purple in extremely clear water.

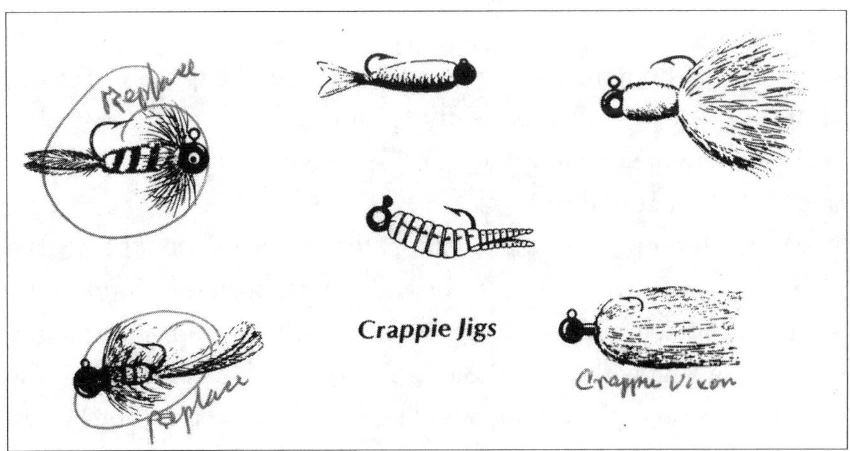

Crappie Jigs

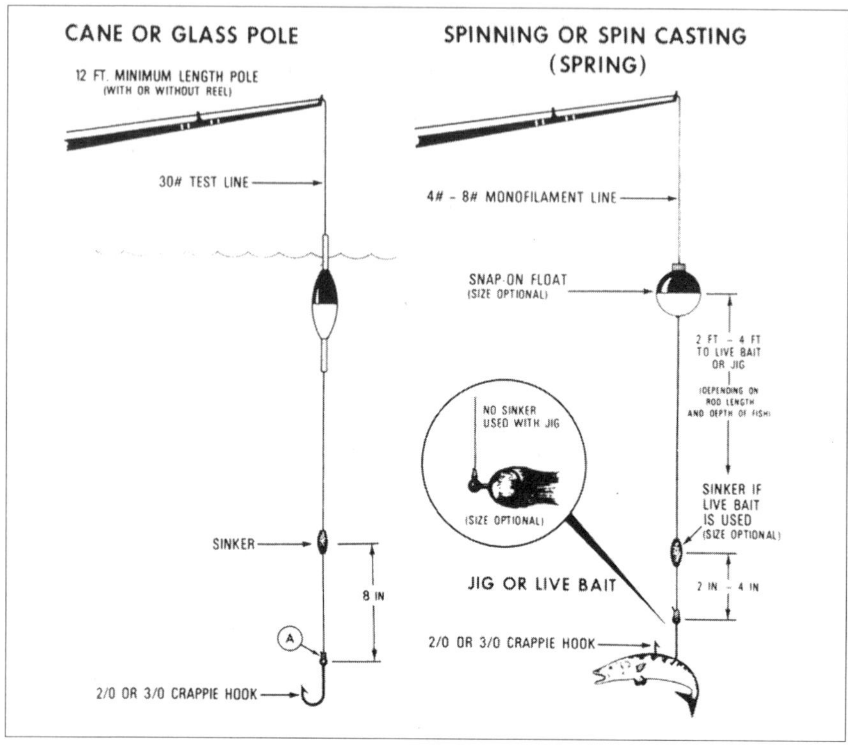

The size of the minnow also varies. A general rule of thumb regarding minnow size might be: small minnows (no longer than two inches) will catch more fish, but when crappies are on a feeding binge, larger minnows will catch larger fish. To this axiom we must add that when crappies are biting sluggishly, smaller minnows will catch more big crappies.

Properly hooking the minnow is important. Crappies can strip a minnow from the hook as stealthily and skillfully as the best pickpocket. Therefore, the minnow must be hooked securely, while taking care that it remains alive.

For still fishing with a plain hook, the minnow should be hooked high in the back, just below the dorsal fin, or through the mouth by inserting the hook into the lower lip and on through the top of the mouth.

For casting with a jig, the minnow can be hooked through the mouth or through the eye sockets. The first is a good technique when

Spinners add that "something extra" to any lure. Nickel-silver and white spinners are favorites among ardent crappie anglers.

fishing in heavy vegetation. The jig-minnow combo is deadly for crappie, but many anglers believe it can be even more effective with the addition of a spinner. The spinner has long been a part of angling, but only in recent years has it received the attention it deserves. It embodies the principle of a blade mounted on a shaft so that it revolves completely.

The spinner creates the illusion of a minnow, or at least something edible, in three ways: it vibrates, it flashes, and it provides motion. Fish do not hear the way we do, nor do they exhibit external ears anything like ours, but fish "feel" sound and vibration. In fact, fish themselves emit vibrations that are "audible" to other fish. Thus, spinners attract fish by the vibrations they create when pulled through the water.

Secondly, when a plain minnow or jig fails to attract crappie, the bright glittering flashes of a spinner will often instigate a strike.

Spinner blades come in various colors such as black, white or yellow, but the polished brass and nickel-silver finishes are most popular. The bright-colored spinners seem to take more crappie, especially in muddy, turbid waters where white crappies are found. A yellow jig with a silver spinner has proven deadly for black crappie in the clear waters of northern lakes and southern and western reservoirs.

While the minnow remains the most popular live bait, there exists an elite corps of panfishermen who swear by the meat system. Meat fishing may consist of either a small strip of pork rind attached to a plain hook or a quarter-inch-wide strip of flesh (about one and one-half inches long) taken from a crappie or other panfish. Be sure to leave the skin attached.

A small minnow-shaped strip of meat cut from the back of a perch or crappie and attached to a no. 6 hook with a silver spinner is deadly. They say it appeals to more of the fish's senses especially smell and taste. Be sure to toss away the strip of meat after catching four or five fish as it seems to lose some of its odor.

Pork rind has been the bass angler's favorite for more than a quarter-century. In most cases, it is not as effective as a minnow for crappie fishing. It does have one advantage, especially when crappie are pecking at the bait—it is virtually impossible for crappie to steal the rind off of a hook.

Crappie baits should be determined by what the fish are striking at the moment. Popular late-summer baits in shallow reservoirs are katydids, grasshoppers, worms, tiny marshmallows, and even corn. The minnow remains the most popular, though the species of minnow varies widely from shiners and small chubs to shad minnows or even small goldfish.

As mentioned earlier, the "complete angler" needs only a handful of equipment to catch crappie. There are, however, any number of extras to enhance your success. A trolling motor enables one to move silently in shallow water without spooking crappie off their spawning beds or away from the protective confines of a brush pile. If you plan a serious pursuit of crappie or largemouth bass, an electric motor is a good purchase.

A depth finder can also be valuable. Crappies are structure fish, meaning they tend to gather around underwater objects such as brush piles, rocky reefs, sunken islands, or old stream channels. A depth finder is especially helpful in locating the submerged structures.

When fishing an unfamiliar lake the crappie angler should have a contour map to help find drop offs and reefs especially if you are without a depth locator. A GPS or GPS pre-programmed maps are extremely helpful.

Crappie fishermen might also consider using two anchors instead of one. Often crappie schools hold along edges of sharp drop-offs. If any wind is present, the boat may pull the anchor down the incline so the craft floats off the spot. Another anchor prevents this from occurring and also keeps the boat in position along the edge of the drop-off.

Another type of anchor worthy of mention is the clamp type used by crappie anglers who work flooded forests. Here, it is simply a matter of clamping the anchor to the nearest stump.

One last note: The tender mouths of crappie can tear off a nylon stringer especially when many fish are put on a small stringer; save those stringers for the big fish—walleye, bass, and pike. Instead keep crappie either in a cloth sack or a wire mesh basket ringed with styrofoam so it will float. If your boat has a live well, even better.

Boat docks hold crappie most of the year if deep water exists nearby. Fish these structures early in the morning and late in the day.

Working the Mexican border reservoir for tree-flooded crappie.

Always crappie can be found under a stump on the shaded side.

Spring to mid-June sees sunken brush piles produce large numbers of huge crappie.

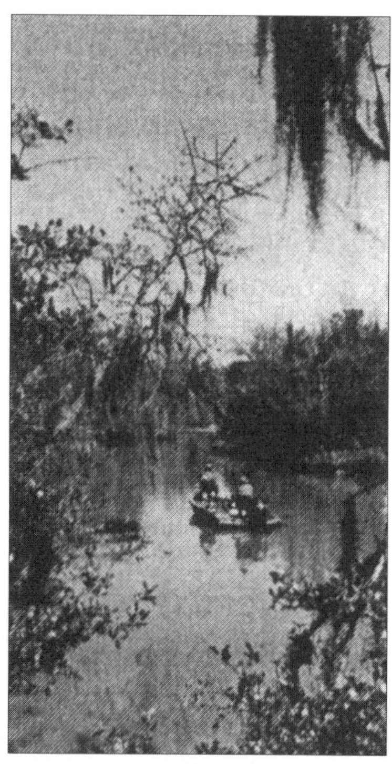

An Alabama backwater produces both crappie and bass.

Chapter Five

The Insect Feeder

Evening sun gleamed golden off the quiet, flat surface of the bay. Lily pads, their edges turning upward, lay deathly still on the still waters. Then, small sucking sounds began to echo towards the jon boat and its two panfish fishermen. The evening feed of bluegill had begun.

Above the lilies, numbers of brown caddis flies began to flit erratically. The hatch was on. Even so, the surface water held quiet. As they often do, the lake's bluegill population was feeding on the caddis larvae climbing their way to surface on the lily stems, inching their way up to hold onto the bottom side of the huge green leaves. Later they'd emerge as adults. The bluegills were nudging up under the pads and sucking the larvae off the underside of the leaves as the insects made their break for freedom. Thus, the soft sucking pops. It was the 'gills inhaling the insects. Soon they'd be feeding on the adult caddis as they came back to the water surface to lay their eggs.

Completion of the insect's lifecycle would take but two hours. It began as the larvae emerged from the soft bottom loam an hour be-

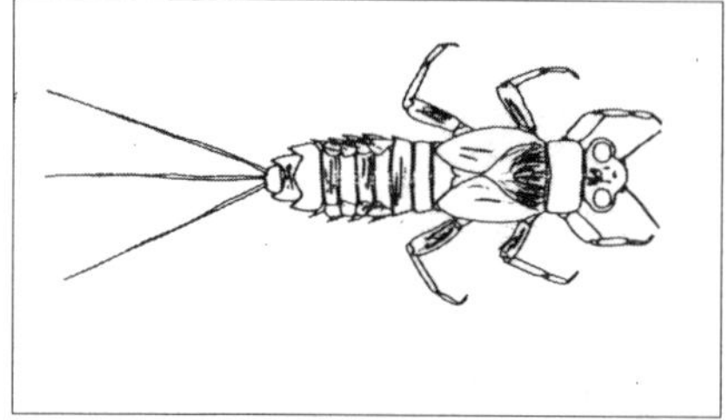

Mayfly larva.

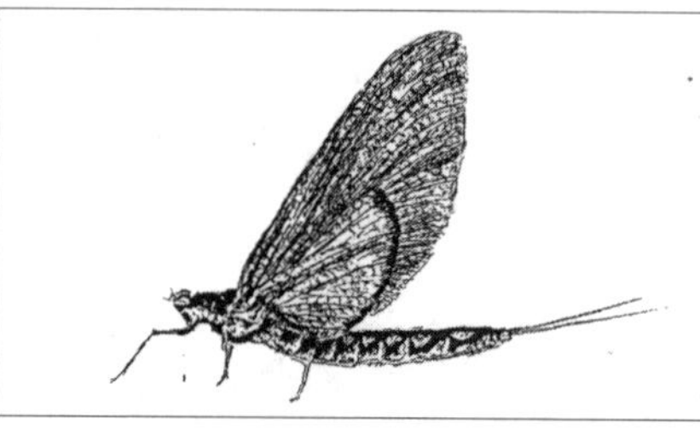

Adult mayfly.

fore. It would end as the insect came to surface later to lay eggs. Not much of an adult life but enough to see the insect's life pattern complete.

Enough to fill the bellies of the fat little bluegill that waited twenty-two hours for the cycle to occur once again. So it would happen each August evening in this tiny micro system of our fishing world.

Knowing the bluegills would savagely attack anything that moved on surface water, small brown dry flies were tied to seven-and-one-half-foot fly rod leaders. At this point, small dimples between the pads and in front (lakeside) of the lily structure began to appear.

Both the anglers cast to a recently appearing dimple of water. Instantly their offering was sucked in with a familiar *pop*. The feed was on and would remain so as long as the hatch continued.

Not until the fisherman in the bow of the boat yelped. He'd set hook into something other than a 'gill.

The fish, its emerald-green back arching above water didn't suck in the insect. Instead he rolled over on it, then gathered it into its large mouth on the rollover.

"Crappie," came the astonished announcement from the bow angler. This hadn't been expected! Then, as if someone had tripped a switch, the backs of the crappies were rolling all around the anglers.

They would add seventeen ten- to twelve-inch silver-sides to the catch of twenty-one hand-sized bluegill.

The two Michigan anglers had stumbled into a common occurrence that happens throughout the country. Once fly hatches begin in earnest, all panfish species will key in on the easy meals. Food in this case triggered the crappie's inner instincts and they had left their deep water sanctuary to take advantage.

Not only crappie can be triggered by feeding bluegills, but perch, goggle-eye, and bass will respond to the call. Then, as nature wills it, pike, muskie, and walleye follow the insect feeders.

There's also a similar happening in late June in many of our lakes, ponds, and backwaters. Minnows by the millions, those of the spring spawn, ripple a quiet lake's surface as weather causes them to gravitate to the surface. Schools of hundreds dart about, foreheads touching the surface. Such actions create a reaction from the panfish below as they migrate to the surface bent on a meal.

It can all begin as the evening sun touches the western shoreline. Instead of dimples and popping sounds, splashes of many sizes disturb the surface. It begins with a bluegill bite, then the crappie, and eventually transfers onto the rest of the fish in the structure.

Gathering these greedy fish is best done by using a tiny crankbait such as a Fish Fry. The one-inch size is preferred. The approach technique used is a simple one. Cast it out and allow it to lie on surface. Then twitch it a couple times, and surely you will raise a strike. Often, you will not even have a chance to twitch it before a bluegill, crappie, or bass sucks it in.

Gear is simple. Use a five- or five-and-one-half-foot ultra-light spinning rod loaded with four-pound mono and a tiny Fish Fry crankbait. Crank color can be just about anything in your box. I like bluegill, shad, and crappie coloring best. Remember crappie and bluegill actually eat their young. Frankly, my experiences have proved that color doesn't matter. As long as your bait is the right size and appears to represent the minnows you're attempting to imitate, it works. With the feeders looking at your offering from the bottom at this time of day, it's my belief they see only the bait's dark silhouette.

If crappie is your game during this time, you'll be pleasantly rewarded to know that crappie biting on this structure may run far into the night, or at least as long as schools of minnows erupt to the surface.

Why do these schools appear during the hot days of summer at this time of day? No biologist has been able to explain the phenomenon to me, but if I were to guess, it may be a connection of things. Surface water temperatures have risen throughout the water structure. These schools of minnows, mostly fatheads, shiners, and game fish spawn from spring have been driven off the two- to twelve-inch water depth of the shoreline by the warm water. This response may see these minnows migrate to water of a similar temperature in the three- to six-foot offshore water which is now on the surface. Or it could be the abundance of food in the form of tiny insect life staged here that is the draw factor. It may be these two factors or some other unknown factors which cause this phenomenon. No matter, if you are a panfish angler it's a happening you should cash in on.

As this chapter has described, equipment is simple and easily gathered. A light seven-and-one-half-foot fly rod or ultra-light spinning outfit should be your weapon of choice. Small #14 to #10 popping bugs or floating flies should be chosen for bait on your fly rod.

Spinning tackle should be loaded with four- to six-pound line and tiny miniature crankbaits no longer than one and one-half inches such as Fish Fry will work best.

Fly-seduced crappie.

Millions of insects and panfish.

Another trick used by some spin anglers is to place a floating fly twelve inches below a bobber. The bobber gives them the weight needed to cast the light fly and does the job of holding the fly near the surface.

Action given to the fly, popper, or Fish Fry crankbait should be kept to a minimum. Let the insect feeder come to you. Too much action deters their desire to strike. Maybe previous generations of panfish have learned through trial and error that too often they miss the food when it moves away just as they strike. Crappie react less from fast actions, while bluegill will back off more readily.

Tip: If you use light spinning gear try using a one-sixty-fourth-ounce Freshwater Shrimp tied to your line twelve inches below a float or bobber. Cut the tail down on the shrimp. This best represents the fly larva now ascending to surface. Use a natural-colored Freshwater Shrimp such as tan, grey, olive, or brown.

Joe Gapen hoists a stringer of Toledo Bend crappie, soon to become a supper meal.

Chapter Six
The Welcome Invasion

Each spring, it begins anew. From sprawling 185,000-acre Toledo Bend Reservoir in Texas to tiny Derby Pond, a fifteen-acre jewel in Delaware, the fever is infectious.

The fever has no regard for age, color, gender, or religion. There is no stopping its inexorable invasion of cities, towns, and farms throughout America. In Yalobusha County near Coffeeville, Mississippi, hundreds are infected and immediately seek a cure at nearby Grenada Reservoir.

Weeks later, Missourians by the thousands are affected and soon they flock to Lake of the Ozarks, where the promised remedy awaits. More than a month later, the epidemic finally begins to wane in the northern tier of states and Canada where anglers gather on crystal-clear waters, spawned by glaciers some 12,000 years ago.

In its wake, the fever has left millions of Americans deliriously happy. Many a delicious meal has been consumed, freezers filled and new memories crowded into the deep recesses of the mind to be recalled and relived, told and retold for years to come.

The annual spring crappie run is a fishing fever that collectively affects more Americans than any other outdoor event. Why is it so popular? Every crappie angler would probably have a unique answer. For most it offers the first chance to wet a line after many months of doing nothing but watching an endless parade of football, basketball and hockey games for excitement.

Now is the chance to compete in person against something, instead of battling an opponent vicariously. Now is the chance to take in the fresh spring air, to see warblers returning from winter homes and to watch migrating arrows of waterfowl pierce the springtime sky.

Like the ducks and geese, crappie also are in the process of migrating—from deepwater haunts to brushy shallows where they will fan out their spawning beds. And once the crappies are bedded fishing begins in earnest.

Throughout the nation a popular spring fishing technique is to anchor or drift through spawning grounds or other areas where crappie are concentrated, casting colorful jigs tipped with small minnows. Meanwhile, shore anglers are dabbling minnows and/or small fly-spinner combinations amid brush piles and fallen trees.

Crappie by the millions are pulled from the nation's waters each spring. But many more, especially of the "lunker" variety, could be caught if the anglers applied some accepted techniques.

A nice catch of black and white crappie.

Crappies are extremely sensitive to disturbance, especially during spawning season. So, when approaching your favorite spot by boat, cut the outboard motor at least fifty yards from the site. Then drift, row or use an electric motor to maneuver into casting position.

Once in position, determine the approximate depth and set your bobber accordingly. A bobber is recommended for this type of fishing because it keeps the lure off the bottom and enables you to keep your bait in the area of crappie concentrations for a longer period of time. The bobber should be small, but colorful, so it can be easily spotted. When in six feet of water, set the bobber about four and one-half to five feet ahead of the hook.

When casting a bobber and several feet of handling line, keep your arm and wrist stiff in order to lob the bait into the air. This type of cast differs from flipping a spoon or rubber worm, which is simply a matter of flicking the wrist. Use a side arm thrust at a forty-five-degree angle from your body.

Many anglers attach a small split shot or bobber stop to their line at the desired level above the bobber. Then attach the float so it can slide freely on the line. Thus, when the rig hits the water, the bobber will slide up to the split shot to stop at the desired depth. Using a rayon cloth knot works best on slick monofilament line.

As your bait and bobber strike the water, count to three to give your bait time to settle. Crappie will often strike anything falling in on top of the school, so be ready! If nothing happens, twitch your rod tip several times in quick succession, wait several more seconds, and then start your retrieve. Retrieve ever so slowly, allowing the bobber on the surface to stop every two feet or so.

A dock, a cane pole, a bobber, and a minnow is all the child needs to push him into a lifetime of fishing.

If you are not using a bobber, maintain some tension on the line as the lure falls. Keep a couple fingers on the line as it flits downward, and, if you feel the telltale thump, set the hook—not hard—but firmly.

The retrieve varies widely from angler to angler. Some maintain a steady return, twitching the rod in quick succession every few seconds. Others reel quickly for several seconds, then allow the bobber to sit quietly, sometimes for ten seconds or longer. These, of course, are the two extremes.

Never retrieve the bait without twitching the rod tip, however, 'jigging' gives a jerky hectic look to the bait, as if it were either wounded or attempting to escape. And there's something about that effect that is deadly on crappie.

Probably the best type of retrieve method, one that is producing fish at that moment, is being exhibited right next to you. Try to emulate the retrieve of successful anglers nearby. Often one type of retrieve will prove more successful than another.

Crappie seldom strike the lure with the gusto of bass or trout. Instead they simply race up, suck it in and then allow themselves to be pulled in. Setting the hook can be accomplished either with a quick snap of the wrist and forearm or simply by tightening the line. As a

Working panfish habitat on an Alabama reservoir.

general rule: when still-fishing, it is best to set the hook. If trolling, drifting or casting, simply tighten the line and start to reel. Always keep in mind the paper-thin moth of a crappie. It will tear easily!

Crappie are not noted for their fighting ability and seldom jump, such as one on the opposite page. However, it doesn't take much for the crappie's soft cartilage to tear. And if the angler fails to keep a taut line, the hook is likely to fall out.

The crappie is not a spectacular battler, but it does fight in tight circles using its flat body to add resistance as it is reeled in. Remember his nickname. "Papermouth" is definitely not a misnomer.

Three important points should be remembered when playing a crappie. First, once the fish is hooked, do not reset the hook or "pump" in the fish. The latter is a common mistake of crappie anglers. Pumping the rod increases the pressure on the hook, which can tear the fragile cartilage of the crappie's mouth. Thus, what started as a tiny puncture soon becomes a gaping hole from which the hook can easily slip out if the crappie turns quickly, or if there is any slack in the line.

Second, keep the line taut. Even without pumping the rod, the hole in the mouth will grow larger as the fish is reeled in. And if the line is slackened, the lure may fall out.

Third is the landing technique. Several methods can be employed here. A landing net probably is the surest method, but not all anglers want to mess with a net when the fishing is fast and furious. Another sure-fire method is to grab the crappie's mouth. This may be difficult and sometimes dangerous in rougher water when you must lean out over the gunwale to grasp a fish.

Another technique used commonly by cane pole fishers and spincasters is simply to hoist the fish into the boat or onto the shore. More fish are lost this way but remains popular because it is fast and easy. To increase your chances of landing crappie by this method, gently raise the rod and swing the fish into the boat like a boom and derrick unloading a ship's cargo.

Do not jerk the fish from the water. By maintaining an even, continuous motion and being careful to lift it smoothly from the water, a crappie is momentarily calmed (like putting a chicken's head under its wing). Seldom, if ever, will it flop during the procedure. Losing half-pounders when they are biting furiously is no big deal. But when that two-pounder falls off into the water, it can be quite upsetting.

Another point to consider when playing this fish is that many experts will not reel in their first crappie, but let it fight out where the school is feeding. Presumably, the action of the hooked fish excites the entire school into a feeding spree, and they may strike the next lure more rapidly.

The preceding pages cover the "basics" of springtime crappie fishing. But there remains a wide array of angling techniques—some simple, some bordering on the bizarre—used throughout the country. Hopefully, you may try some of these innovative methods on your favorite lake or stream. What works in one region might also work somewhere else.

. . . *Don't flip fish into the boat!*

Don't reel fish to top of your pole!

DO slowly lift and swing fish into the boat!

TAKE YOUR CHILD FISHING!

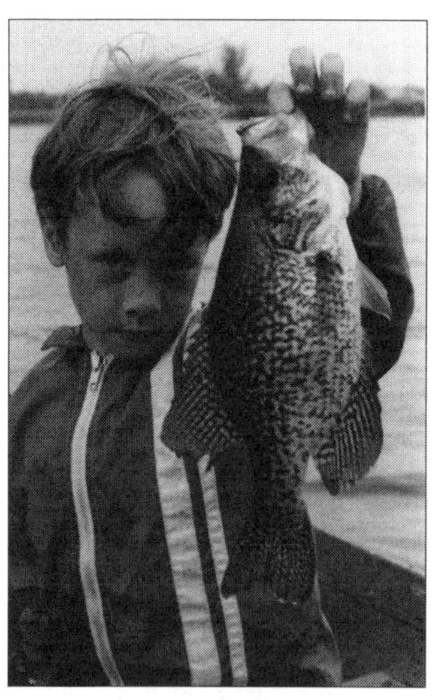

Anglers in the southern reservoirs of Virginia, Mississippi, Kentucky, and Tennessee use cane poles and forty- to fifty-pound monofilament line to angle for crappie over sunken logs, flooded forests and brush piles. Attached to the line is a thin wire hook that bends easily when pulled from a snag. Once the hook is tugged free, it is reshaped, baited again, and fishing resumes.

The cane pole is the long arm of the spring bank angler. Crappie fishing experts walk along the edges of reservoirs in search of brush piles—and crappie. This entails nothing more than fishing brush piles ten to fifteen feet from shore in three to eight feet of water.

Many old sages "fix" their own hotspots by dropping willow trees into the water. Within a matter of days, crappie will invade the spot, and the angler is assured of another hefty stringer.

Another spring technique is "bed-fishing." The angler locates reed-laden shallows where crappies are on their beds, and then drifts or silently paddles a boat or canoe in search of fish.

A quiet sunny day when wind does not exceed five miles per hour or a quiet out-of-the-wind cove makes this type of fishing possible. Scan the shallows for spawning crappie. When a fish is sighted, lower a minnow hooked on a small #8 hook in front of the guarding male crappie or directly over its bed. You have the advantage because you can see the fish take the bait and immediately set the hook. Some anglers use shorter rods or even ice fishing jig sticks to effectively maneuver the bait into position.

This practice has generated some controversy. It is argued the parent fish should not be removed from guarding the freshly deposited eggs or fry. But fishery managers assure us that heavy fishing pressure over spawning beds seldom does anything to adversely affect a lake's crappie population.

Another tried-and-true technique for catching spawning crappie from Texas to Minnesota is reed fishing. Anglers either from shore or in boats move silently past reed beds carefully scanning the brush for any trembling reeds or stickups. Spotting any movement may mean a crappie is just below the reed busily fanning its nest.

Incidentally, during spring most anglers concentrate their fishing efforts on the nest-guarding male crappie. However, immature males and lunker females waiting to spawn in early spring may be found out from shore in ten to as much as thirty feet of water. The key to finding these fish is to locate weed beds just off sheer drop-offs. These deep, sunken, last year's weed growths provide prespawn cover for crappies.

Young Minnesota anglers flock to a rain-swollen lake to catch limits of crappie off a favorite dock.

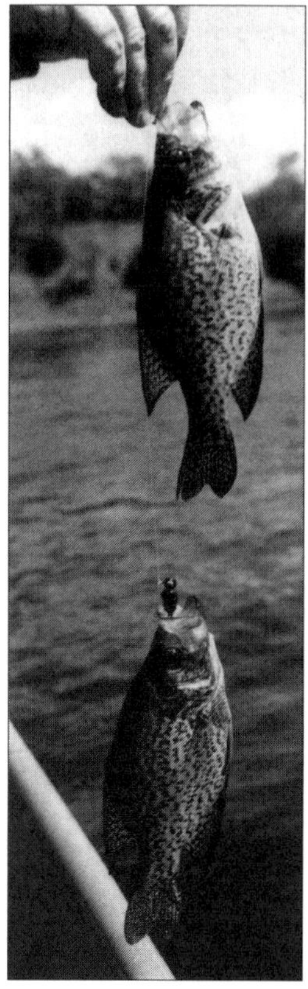
A double rig will often pro-
duce double catches.

Spring is when countless anglers turn to night fishing, especially for huge slab crappie. Along and under bridges and in the brushy shallow flats of southern reservoirs, entire cities of boats light up the night. It seems crappie guard their nests even more actively at night and will attack any bait thrown in the vicinity of their nests.

Armed with flashlights and lanterns, Louisiana anglers by the hundreds head out on Friday and Saturday evenings to set their yo-yos. The yo-yo is a mechanical device which will automatically set the hook and hold the crappie until the angler can arrive and boat it.

The yo-yo earned its name because of its resemblance and action similar to the toy enjoyed by so many youngsters. The yo-yo is a spring-loaded reel with several feet of line housed on a spool. To set it for action, line is pulled from the spool to place the hook at the desired depth. This compresses a spring powering the reel or spool, which winds in the line following the strike.

The device can even play a large fish, yielding line as the fish tugs hard, retrieving line as the fish tires. Eventually it will wear down even a very large crappie.

Yo-yos are usually attached to tree limbs by means of twine. In open water there are few trees, so it is a common practice to string a number of devices on a long line, similar to a trotline, suspended just above the water. Several early studies, however, have shown the device to be somewhat ineffective for taking fish in wide open waters.

More has been written about springtime angling than any other phase of crappie fishing. It can be exciting and productive. But unfortunately, the spring crappie fishing bonanza is short lived with the entire spawning run lasting only a few weeks.

After spring crappie fever is gone, anglers turn their attention to other species, such as bass, walleye, sunfish, and pike. But excellent crappie angling lies ahead, though fishing won't be as easy. Where do crappies go once they leave the shallows? When is the best time to fish them? Should I switch solely to still-fishing with minnows? The answers to these questions and much more awaits you in the following chapters.

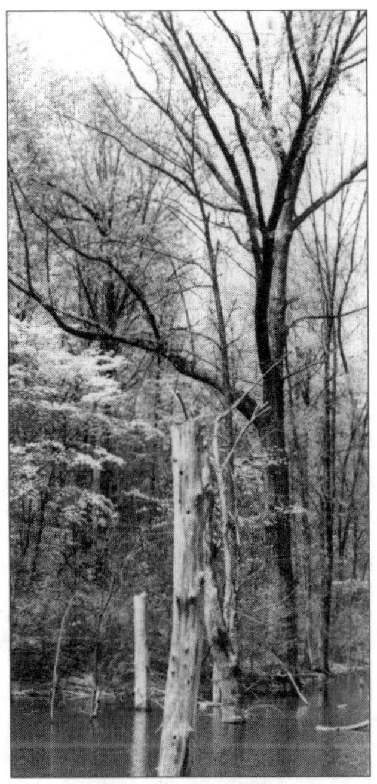

Panfish Structure
Deadwood, flooded trees, and dogwood blossoms create an enticing structure that draws panfish.

Secret Panfish Tips for New Anglers:

No. 1. With a paper-thin mouth, crappies require little or no effort when setting the hook. If fishing with a bobber, a steady lift upwards is all that is needed as the float disappears.

No. 2. Crappies are a vertical riser as they ingest food. That is the reason granddad's turkey quill float worked so well. Granddad would rig the quill with just enough weight to see it submerge much of the float. Then, as the crappie ingested the bait, he would rise up about six inches, which caused the quill to rise up and lay flat on the water surface. All the angler had to do was lift his fishing rod and swing the captured fish into the boat.

No. 3. Instead of a fast lift into the boat or attempting to hand-land a crappie, try a gentle lift and swing it into the boat instead. Such action prevents tearing the hook out of the thin mouth of this fish.

No. 4. Bluegill, red ears, and bream spawn after crappie and often use the same bed used by the crappie. One other benefit of this spawning technique is that bluegill feed on the crappie eggs and hatch near at hand. Therefore, if you know where the crappie beds are in your lake, it's an easy trick to locate the 'gills as they reproduce.

No. 5. When looking for summer deep-water crappie, keep in mind they haven't just disappeared. They have schooled up after the spawn, retreated into deeper water, generally at a depth of fifteen feet to over twenty to twenty-five feet of depth. One of the reasons crappie are so hard to find is that they continually go into a search migration for minnow schools.

Crappie show up as a blob on your locator, a blob which doesn't stay put. One sure way to find these wanderers is to slip bob the lakesides of cabbage weeds that grow in about fourteen feet of depth. These schools will travel a hundred feet or so out into the main lake off this structure and crappie close in on the weeds in search of minnows just at sundown or shortly after daylight.

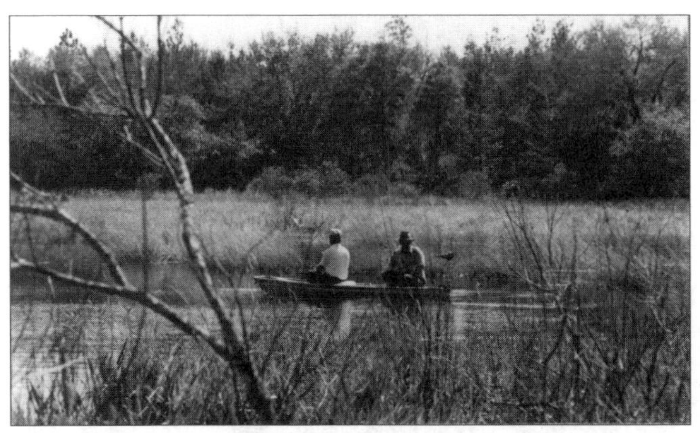

Chapter Seven
Special Spring Spots

Lloyd Volmer is a special friend of mine . . . not because he's one of southern Minnesota's better crappie fishermen, but mainly because Lloyd is just one hell of a guy. We've fished together many times over the years, some days good, some bad. Take the time Lloyd had too many snorts of moo juice and ran the press pontoon boat over our state's governor's line! That wasn't that bad, but what *was* bad was that Governor Anderson had his first walleye of the day nearly up to net. That took place many years ago, and since them my friend has seen the light. He no longer indulges in the pursuit of mind-blurring grain juices. But he does continue to enjoy catching panfish far above all other fishes. When it come to crappie fishermen, I've met few any better.

During spring, prior to publication of the revised edition of *A Fish for All Seasons . . . Crappie*, my old friend and I once again found ourselves invited to the Minnesota Governor's Opening Day Fishing event. We were instructed that fishing must be done within an area in a section of southern Minnesota's farm country. That meant walleyes would be small and come hard. The official fishing opener began at midnight on Friday evening. Final weigh-in would come Sunday afternoon at 4:00 p.m. It would be two full days of fishing for too-small walleye with not many bites in between.

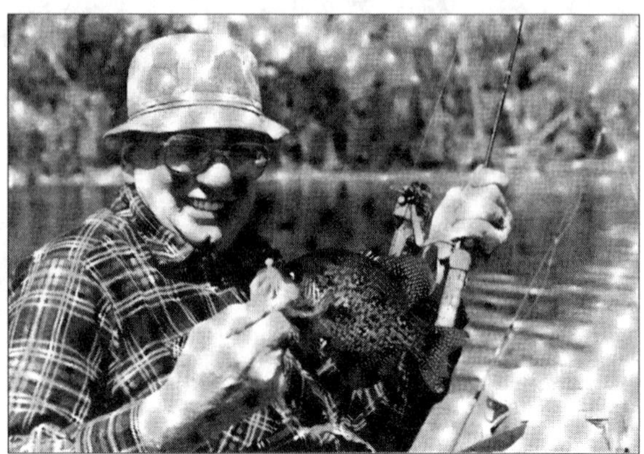

Lloyd Volmer proudly displays average spring-caught black crappie.

"Dan, the crappies are really hot west of here on a lake near my home. It's a bit out of our designated territory, but no one will know," the ever-devious Lloyd mentioned at supper on Friday night.

The thought of catching pound-size walleye didn't thrill me. There'd be more than enough fishing pros at the governor's party who'd enjoy such fish. But pound-size crappie did excite me!

"They're up in shallow water . . . about three to four feet, and we've been taking them on light jigs suspended under a small bobber," Lloyd added fuel to the fire.

As tradition dictated, Lloyd and I opened that night at midnight on a small lake where there was a possibility of taking a big walleye. No such luck. Sunrise found us with four fish a bit better than the half-pound average expected. Our biggest touched the two-pound mark on Lloyd's scale.

"Had enough of this nonsense, partner?" I grunted as we headed in for breakfast.

He had. After breakfast, it was off to the secret lake where spawning spring crappies were known to gather.

Madison Lake, the lake Lloyd and I would fish, is like many farm country lakes in central North America. It stands relatively shallow, contains a bit of surface rock along shoreline where noticeable points break towards open water and for the most part, has a sandy bottom. In bay waters, depths seldom reach more than ten feet and are almost always weedy in one manner or another. If deep water exists, it does so more toward the lake's center or far off shore's existing points.

In Madison Lake's northeastern corner, there is a shallow bay notorious for spring crappie. It was here Lloyd would guide our boat after breakfast. Time registered 8:20 a.m. as we departed dockside.

"At the far end, along the left side, a sandbar juts out and across the bay. It's here we've been taking the crappie in and among those dead rush and stem weeds left from last year," Lloyd instructed as we slowly motored into the shallow bay.

"If you don't have any small one-sixteenth-ounce white fox hair Crappie Vixen jigs and Marabou Freshwater Shrimp along, I have plenty. Place a small float, about five-eighths-inch in diameter, some three feet above the jig and get ready. We're just about there!" my guide

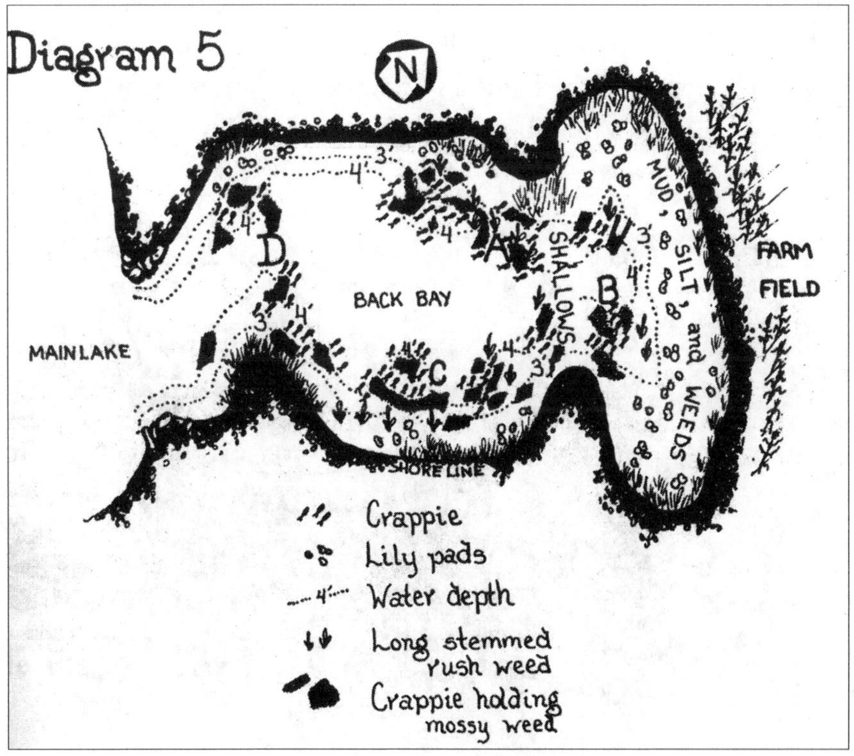

further instructed as the motor slowed even more and we headed in toward a rush-covered point.

Lake water was clear enough to see bottom in about three feet. Careful examination could even produce a dim sighting of bottom in some four-foot depths. Especially visible were the dead and decaying clumps of rush and weed stems from last year. They stood out as protruding black/brown smudges seemingly suspended in the gloomy water. It was also noted that these dead, broken and dying weeds had collected a parasite of soft moss that held suspended around and through the entire structure of weeds. I had seen this same condition many other places while fishing for early crappie. Yessir, this was crappie country.

Adding to my conviction, every once in a while I noted a slowly darting black fish form that would move this way or that as boat bow shifted.

"Crappie! Black . . . and good 'uns!"

Lloyd knew what he was talking about. They were here . . . here in goodly numbers if the sightings I now experienced were any indicator. In a hundred yards, I counted three dozen fish flushed by our boat.

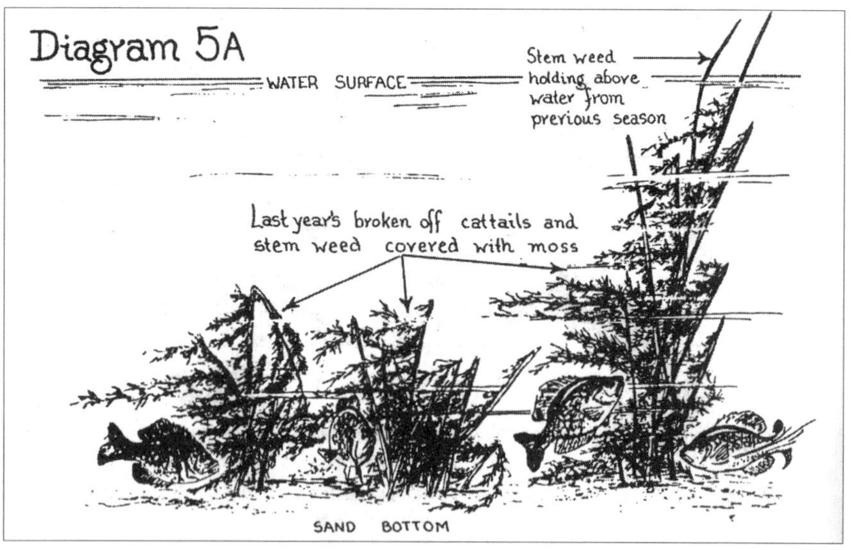

"We're passing over a lot of fish, Lloyd. They look like good fish! I'm ready anytime you are," this anxious passenger noted.

With my comment, Lloyd cut the motor. Our boat glided a few feet and settled at the spot marked A on the diagram on page 51. We had arrived at this point after a zigzag course along the bay's shallow northern shore.

"You ready, Dan?" queried my companion as he cast his first offering. I hadn't even rigged the bobber yet, so excited had I been to see the fish below us.

"Right behind you, Lloyd. You better get one quick or you'll lose the bet on first fish," I coun tered while scrambling through my tackle box in an attempt at finding a bobber of proper size.

"Fish on!" yelped Lloyd.

Sure enough, only moments after placing his jig and bobber combo next to a protruding weed stem, the bobber disappeared, and Lloyd brought the first thrashing crappie to the boat.

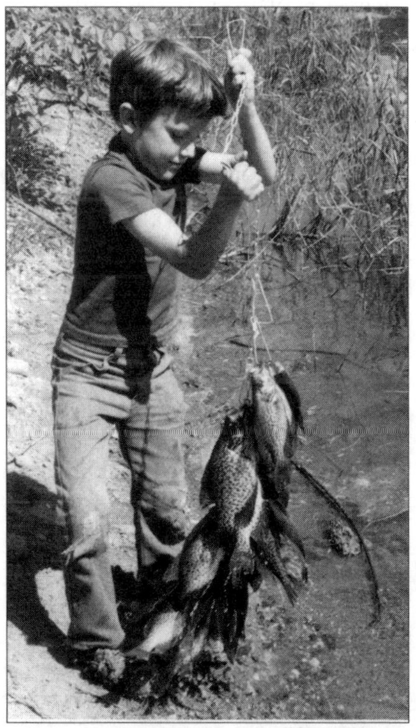

Spring crappie, which hold to the dead weedlines from the year before, are easily caught by all members of the family as this young fellow astests.

Examination of the fish proved it to be a black crappie male of about three-quarters-pound size . . . a real nice fish for a male.

"Your turn, Gapen," laughed Lloyd as another cast was made.

By this time I had the bobber rigged, and I too let loose, aiming my cast at another dark group of weed mass below water. Both jig and bobber landed directly above the dead weeds. And before I could adjust their position, slightly to one side of the underwater weed structure, the bobber disappeared. With a slow returning motion of rod tip, I set hook. It was my turn. A large, pound-plus female darted this way and that but eventually slapped her way across the surface to be swung into our boat.

"This one should have been the first fish, Lloyd. She's much more deserving of winning the dollar, seeing she's twice as big as yours," I needled my guide.

He didn't hear me. Another fish was about to come dancing across the boat bow.

To understand better what is meant by rotted off rush and weed stems from last year and the parasite mosses that frequent such weeds, look to Diagram 7A on page 52. During the previous summer, these low-in-the-water structures were tall rush and pencil-type weeds that rose far above the water surface. But, because of winter ice and natural year-end deterioration of such vegetation, only the root stumps plus a few broken-off stems remain. There is always an exception to the rule as noted in the diagram. Note the right side where pencil weeds still remain above the surface.

These stems that remain are few and far between but can be used by the angler as locating beacons. They soon fall away as new growth begins at plant bottom, but, in the meantime, a smart angler will utilize these above-water remnants as locators by which to spot the better crappie beds.

It is a well-known fact among diehard crappie fanatics that the mouth of a pre- or post-spawn crappie has little, if any, sensitivity. The same might be said for its sense of smell. These facts continue to be an arguing point for many biologists when referring to this fish.

However, from this author's point of view, experiences noted during this spring spawning time only strengthen such facts. I have seen crappie pick up and carry about an eighth-ounce jig for as long as a minute. Considering there was no scenting, natural or manmade on the jig, one might assume it wasn't a sense of smell that caused the fish to hold it in his mouth . . . nor was it the natural feel of the hard foreign material of an artificial jig that fooled the fish.

To further back up my claim that crappie have little or no ability to smell of feel, they are easily taken on plain white, yellow or chartreuse jigs during spring spawn. As summer comes on, this fish becomes more critical of what they'll eat and seldom strike a stationary jig suspended below a bobber unless it has been tipped with a minnow. They will take jigs but only those kept in constant motion by the angler.

These facts enabled Lloyd and me to rig our lines in the manner in which we did.

For a jig we chose a one-sixteenth-ounce round-headed fox hair and marabou jig that housed just a bit of mylar tinsel along its body and down its fluffy tail. The head was painted solid white with a white chenille body and white marabou tail. Thirty-two inches above the jig, we placed a small, five-eighth-inch round plastic red-and-white bobber. This may have been substituted for a six-inch pencil bobber if we had so desired. In our case, neither of us had taken along any pencil bobbers. Thusm the use of the old-fashioned type.

In itself, this rigging may be no different from any others that you, the reader, might have used. However, we did do one thing differently. It was the way we tied jig to line that can make the difference.

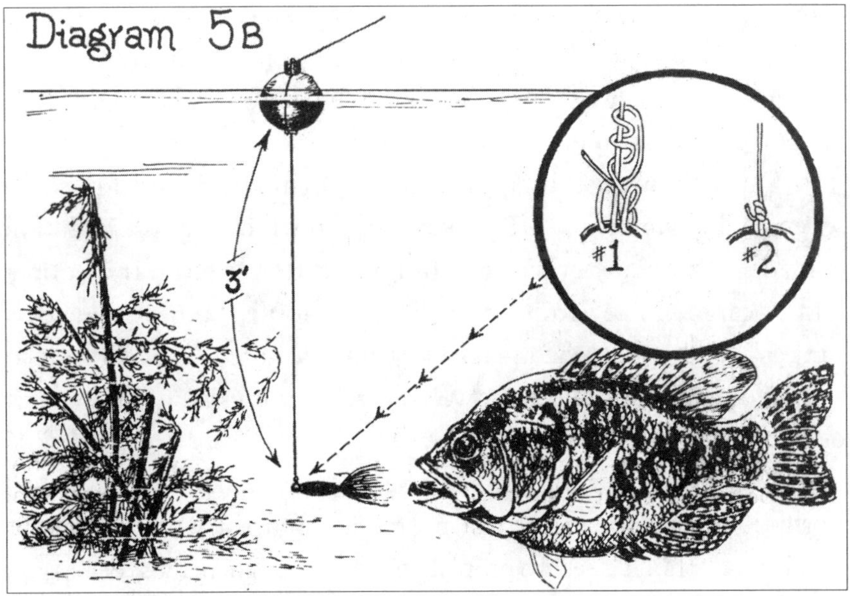

Point: If a jig is simply tied to the line and allowed to hang at any angle, there can be a reduction in fish hits by as much as fifty percent. If, however, you tie the jig so it hangs level to the bottom, your fish hits will dramatically improve. Why?

It's a simple matter of presenting your bait in a natural fashion. Crappies are minnow feeders. A jig is meant to look like a minnow. If it hangs from a line in an unnatural fashion it only makes sense that it will not be as enticing to fish as it would be in a natural swimming minnow position. That means the jig should sit horizontal to bottom or at a right angle to the suspended line beneath the bobber.

One of the easiest and strongest knots to use in tying on small jigs is the double clinch. See diagram 7B for proper tie and rigging directions.

The knot that holds the jig firmly at a right angle is done in a similar manner to the tying of a simple clinch knot but with one improvement. Instead of a simple go around the eye shank, make an extra pair of loops in and out of the eye. This maneuver places a supporting run of line on either side of the original eye-looping line. When tightened, these twin outer loops tighten firmly on the center vertical line, pinching it in towards the center from either side. This in turn places equal pressure, rigidly holding the knot from slipping either way. Thus the jig is held in a horizontal position to the bottom or at a right angle to the descending line.

One of the most disciplined things an angler must learn to do when challenging crappie is the manner in which lure presentation is made. Unlike any other jig fishing, *no* action is given the bobber and its cargo. Once your cast is made, providing you have selected a proper spot for fish, the angler must not move the bait. Allow it to sit stationary for as much as two to three minutes before moving it elsewhere.

The strike of a crappie will not be felt, only seen. Your bobber will slowly disappear in a smooth flowing motion. Once down, the rod tip is lifted and the hook is set. To properly fight crappie, there must be tension kept on the line at all times and a steady retrieve toward the boat is necessary. As the fish comes to the surface, continue to keep it coming, even if it now rests on top. With the same steady flowing action, lift it into the boat or waiting landing net. The reasoning behind this is the paper-thin mouth tissue of this fish. Hooks easily rip large holes along its sides and disengage themselves during battle to break clear.

By referring to Diagram 7 the reader will see a number of excellent spawning areas for crappie. The diagram of this bay is being used because it is typical of spring crappie water.

At Point B, in water depth between three and four feet, similar conditions to those at Point A are found. Only here, the fish are as far into the bay proper as you will find them. It also should be noted that a point protrudes from the south shore forming structures to hold fish. To the left of B, more pencil and rush underwater weed structure is found. Once again, crappie should be there.

At point C, a shallowing not noted on the shoreline is seen. But, a crafty angler is able to detect this crappie-holding area by looking for and spotting the few remaining pencil weeds as they protrude above the surface. Where you find them there will be the clumps of last year's rush and stem weed base which spawning fish seem to love.

On either side of D, an underwater point is indicated. On the south shore, the observer knows it's there by looking to shoreline structure. On the north shore, they would find the underwater point only by spotting the telltale pencil weeds above surface.

Often the angler can find the underwater blobs of deep weed roots and stems where crappies spawn by finding cattails hugging the shoreline. Where they grow along the shore, there is a good chance that others will surely flourish further out in the lake.

It should also be noted that not always will you find crappie-holding weeds along a bay's shoreline just because it's shallow. Look to the north shore of our bay in Diagram 7. Where the shoreline runs straight for a given distance, there may be any underwater structure on which crappie may be found.

Lloyd and I caught a basketful of crappie that day. Most averaged near a pound in weight. That's a nice crappie in anybody's book! Back at the governor's weigh-in, we were greeted with a lot of envious questions. The fishing pros had caught their walleye all right. Most of them didn't have a limit of fish that could outweigh the same number of crappie taken out of our bag at random.

Since that Governor's Opener, I've not had the pleasure of fishing with my old friend, Lloyd Volmer. To the best of my knowledge the tough old character passed on to a better fishing ground. If it's true as rumor has it, I'm sure the giant panfish, especially crappie are taken a beating as spring rolls around each year.

Lloyd taught me much over the years we fished together. It was he who taught me to hunt the dark forms of darting panfish before beginning my quest. At times Lloyd would allow his old tin boat to drift directly over to beds to sight out the bedding fish and register the size of their beds and where the most beds were. Once he even dropped a marker buoy on the largest concentration of crappie beds. While doing this, he mentioned that I shouldn't worry—crappie engaged in the reproductive process couldn't be driven off their beds. "Sort of like young fellas!" He chuckled.

He was right! The interruption of the marker buoy never seemed to chase those spawning crappie off their beds. The buoy then became a mark to which we could cast our bobber presentation.

A lite spinning rod and reel, a Slip-N-Lock Crappie Float and a chartreuse Freshwater Shrimp do the trick on spring bedding crappie.

CRAPPIE . . . A FISH FOR ALL SEASONS AND ALL PEOPLE

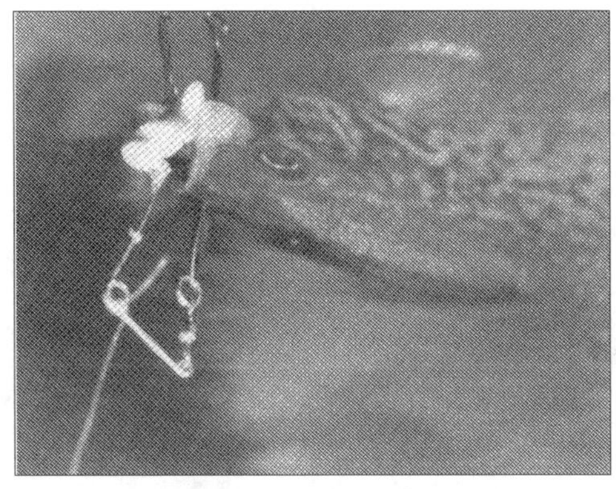

Jig-spinner crappie comes to boat.

Inspection of a netted beauty.

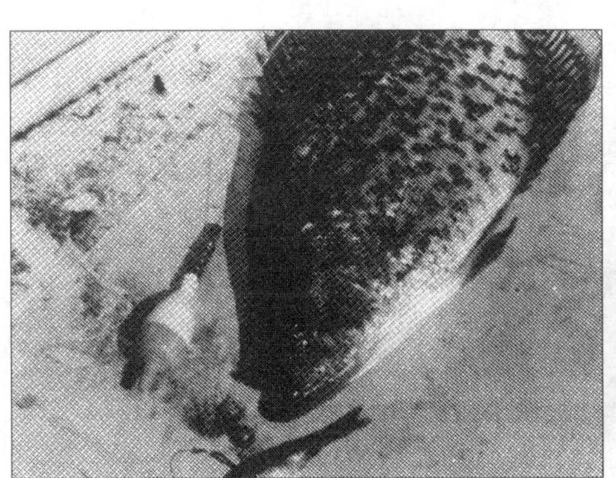

The ol' minnow/float combo is still hard to beat.

Who wouldn't have been proud?

Chapter Eight
A Crappie Cousin

BLUEGILL

Call them what you want—bluegill, bream, stumpknocker, Red Ears or just "The Panfish," this fellow ranks extremely high in the ratings of the true American angler, especially the young ones.

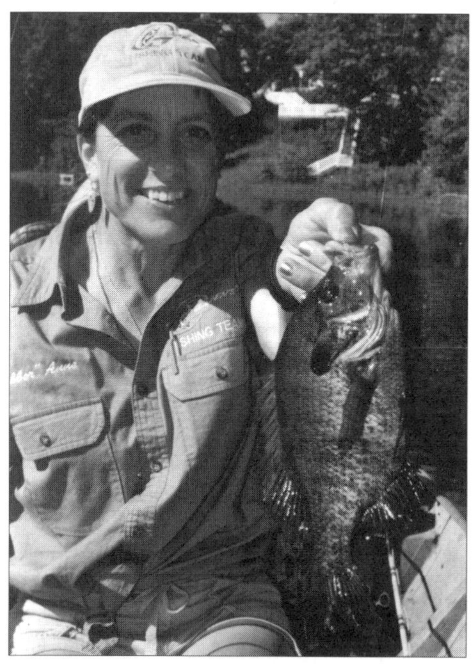

He's easy to catch, aggressively seeks out just about any small natural bait offered to him and ounce for ounce puts up a fight like no other freshwater fish that swims.

Years ago I had a knowledgeable biologist tell me, "If bluegill grew to ten pounds or more, the freshwater angler would be hard pressed to find fishing gear that would conquer him." There's a similar expression describing a wood weasel. The story goes, "If weasels grew to ten or twenty pounds, no man or beast would be safe from this creature when they entered the woods."

It's true. The round structure of a bluegill is put to all its fighting use as this fish fights its angling opponent in a side-darting action to prevent capture. In the two-pound range, ounce for ounce this fellow will outfight any freshwater fish out there.

Like its cousin the crappie, bluegills prefer shallow water structures such as weeds, deadwood, stumps, dead rushes, or flooded willow. In the spring, a time to reproduce, the bluegill will seek out rough sand and gravel texture close to weed growth in which to spawn. Often, because they spawn at a couple degrees water temperature higher than crappie, they often settle on the bed structures recently used by crappies.

Unlike crappies, bluegills may only lay half as many eggs. Even so, half of a hundred thousand is still an enormous amount. Unlike their cousin, bluegill have been known to reproduce twice a year if water conditions are right. This makes this panfish equally as prolific as any of its panfish cousins.

There's no need to worry about taking the bluegill "off its bed" in the spring. Within hours, another "eager-to-spawn" bluegill will replace it. Like all its cousins, taking spawning adults off their beds doesn't harm the population.

If you've ever released a bluegill at this time of year and follow it as it swims away, it always goes back to the bed you took it from. So intent is this fish on reproduction that I've experienced taking the same gill off its bed five times in a row. So protective is this fish of its nest that anything you drop into it will be swept up and spit out on the bed's outer edge each time you place the object back into the bed. This includes split shot, lead sinkers, artificial jigs or natural bait. I once placed a piece of nightcrawler in a 'gill's bed only to have it lifted out and placed outside the nest three times. On my fourth try, as if disgusted with the juicy intruder, the large female completely ingested my offering, which lead to a hookup. Knowing this, the angler has a big advantage over this species of fish.

In late spring, the larger 'gills migrate offshore into deeper water. They leave behind the smaller members of their family to roam the shallow water like schools of small red-bellied piranha. Here they'll stay in one to three feet of water until the hot sun of summer and the rising water temperatures drive them further out into deeper water.

Working panfish in lilypads and reeds.

The larger bluegills, the year's spawners, have now taken up positioning on the first growth of lake weeds. These usually grow in eight to twelve feet of depth. Here the large fish feed on small minnows, insect larvae and any invertebrate they can find. They'll hold here until food runs out or the hot sun of mid-summer drive them even deeper.

At this time, they hold in deep water, and the angler finds bluegill hard to find. Often a large trophy bluegill, a two-pounder, is caught by a walleye angler slipping a black leech across a rocky gravel structure in twenty-four feet of water. The harvest of this prize always comes as a pleasant surprise, but in most cases is never followed up by a second fish.

If the walleye angler had followed up his walleye presentation, he might have scored big on deep-water summer bluegill. But, intent on finding walleye, he carries on out over the reef in pursuit of his table fare.

That's right! Big bluegill can be found in deep water as deep as forty feet, schooled up on the edges of hardpan reefs where the reef plunges deeper. Generally, they hold tightly in a pocket no longer than six feet across. Here, you may find as many as forty to fifty fish. Keep in mind: bluegill are a school fish. No matter where you find them, they'll be herded closer together. The other tip that should have been learned by the walleye pursuer is that deep-water bluegill love leeches. Retracing the troll or float with another leech presentation sometimes produces another trophy bluegill.

One exception to the school theory on big 'gills occurs when these schooled fish depart from their deep water structure as the mayfly hatch begins. Still in deep water, this pod of bluegill will swim off the protection of the deep-water reef edge to intercept the mayfly larvae as it ascends upward toward the surface. At this time the 'gills scatter and stage at eighteen to twenty feet over twenty to thirty feet of depth. Now, instead of being held to a school pattern, they fan out, allowing several feet between each of them to intercept the ascending nymphs.

Once an old friend of mine, Paul Vinton, and I were fishing bass on a lake called Monroe in central Wisconsin when he spotted numerous large red sightings on our Humminbird LCR locator. Finally, after several tries with a one-sixteenth-ounce Freshwater Shrimp I managed to hook one of these unidentified fish. It was a fat red-breasted sunfish that tipped the scales at two pounds one ounce.

Because the red markings were all between eighteen to twenty feet, we decided to use a slip bobber with a tan colored one-thirty-second-ounce Freshwater Shrimp jig. The bass quest was immediately forgotten.

Within an hour, we'd collected nineteen of these beauties, averaging just under two pounds. It turned out to be a lesson I never forgot and have implemented a number of times whenever the mayfly hatch is on. Each application has proved successful. The other lure that works well at this time is a one-thirty-second-ounce Ugly Bug jig. I always use a slip-n-lock balsa float to work the artificial jig whether it be a Freshwater Shrimp or an Ugly Bug.

Fall may be the toughest time to work bluegill and crappie which have retreated even deeper in the water. Refer to Chapter 2 in this book for one solution. Here is another!

Bottom-hugging panfish.

Each fall, as leaves turn yellow, orange, and red, often cold north-west winds descend out of Canada and a strange tactic to produce bluegill and black crappie comes into play. I first learned about this technique on Lake Kabetogama in 2001 while producing a TV show on fall walleye.

"Bobber" Anne, myself, and Dan Keith, the cameraman, had ventured into a large northeastern arm of the big lake that borders Canada and the United States. Here, as before, we expected to pick up good-sized walleye.

"Have you noticed, Dan, the numerous red blotches scattered on the black loam bottom at the twenty-four- to twenty-six-foot mark?" questioned my partner, Anne.

Every four to six feet, the locator was signaling fish hugging the bottom. There seemed to be no space between the fish and the flat bottom. Knowing this portion of the bay had a black loam bottom, I surmised these were rough fish, suckers, bullheads, or carp. Their positioning certainly wasn't that of walleye.

Seeing our fishing so far had been spotty, we all decided to try these belly-bottom-bumping fish. Maybe they were walleye. Such a try would require that we drift slowly, allowing our jig and minnow presentations to gently touch bottom as they were dragged on or nearly on the bottom.

Anne and the cameraman would use the old reliable method of a quarter-ounce chartreuse jighead tipped with a two-inch fathead minnow. I'd use a quarter-ounce chartreuse Ugly Bug also tipped with a minnow.

A soft northwest wind rippled the surface, an ideal wind for drifting. As we passed over a set of marks on the locator screen, Anne's rod tip went down. Moments later, without much fight, she brought a fat pound-and-a-half black crappie to net.

Recently the suspended schools of Kabetogama's black crappie had all but disappeared. Without knowing it, we'd happened on to the structure they'd disappeared to. The belly of Anne's fat fish was stained in patches of black, possibly caused by their positioning with their bellies in the loam.

Any of you who have touched black loam will have discovered it is soft and fluffy to the touch. When disturbed, it sends up a black cloud that soon settles.

Moments later I set hook into an identical crappie. The strike, if it could be called a strike, was more of a gentle pull down of the rod tip. These fish seemed to be sucking in our offerings as the jig minnow combos were slowly dragged past them. It was unlike any other feeding habit of a crappie, but similar in many ways. All of a sudden we had fish on as our rod tips settled slowly downward.

Within an hour, we'd captured seventeen nice fat fall crappie, between a pound and two pounds and a couple fat bluegill. Our TV show had switched its purpose from walleye to panfish and was well on its way to completion as we ended the day. The wind had switched directly to the north and now blew fifteen to twenty miles an hour, too fast for drifting. We would return in the evening as the wind velocity decreased to accomplish the slow drift.

The next day we returned, and success was once again ours. In three days, we managed to boat nearly one-hundred black crappie, all very nice fish, and a dozen fat one-pound bluegill. Accidently we discovered a new way to find fall panfish and a new structure to which they migrated.

The question arose as inspection of the fish's stomach coloring stood out. Why were they here? All, some more so than others, had blackened bellies caused by the natural black dye in their resting of bellies in the loam bottom. Food had to be the draw, but what was the food? The answer came when it was discovered their stomachs held hundreds of tiny freshwater shrimp-like insects. The color of these tiny insect-like critters was black and gray.

Though a minnow feeder by nature, these crappie had found an easier protein source to follow up on for winter. For the bluegill, insect larva are a main portion of their diet throughout the year.

Since that outing, I've applied the lessons learned that cold October day in various regions of our fishing world at different times of the fall, all with success.

Once on Reelfoot Lake in late fall, I found the lake's bluegill and crappie holding on deep-water structure on muddy bottom doing a similar thing. So, you panfish guys may want to apply these techniques when the bellies of the crappie you boat show up with dark staining on them.

The moral of this tip is that the famous minnow feeder doesn't always feed on minnows, but when offered one, even though he's feeding on insects, he will take it.

Panfish cousins.

Chapter Nine

Summer—Hot Fishing in Cool Places

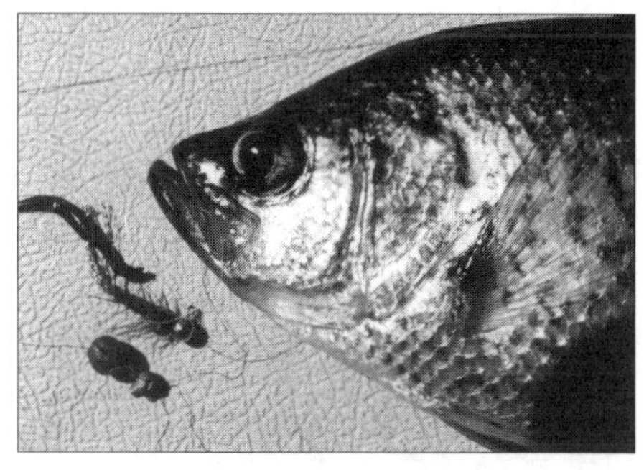

Split Shot, a Freshwater Shrimp, and a leech for hot summer panfish.

It was a typical summer day—hot and humid with a gentle breeze providing fleeting moments of relief. For the past week, our walleye fishing on the pine-studded northern lake had been excellent. Two nine-pound fish had already been netted along with numerous "Minnesota-size" walleyes—those in the one-and-one-half- to two-and-one-half-pound bracket.

But now, on our last day on this lake, walleye fishing had tapered off. Our depth locators continued to blip the big schools of walleye over jutting rock shelves and sandbars, but no amount of coaxing would induce a strike.

Toward evening, I reluctantly decided to abandon walleyes for largemouth bass. The breeze was now a faint whisper as I anchored at the edge of a large weed bed about 150 feet from shore. The water below was a tapestry of tall green weeds that rose over fifteen feet to tickle the surface.

A fly rod was first put into play and for the next half hour a large green popper bounced and sputtered across the water. Nothing! Switching to an open-face spinning reel, I tied on a small yellow-hair jig, attached a lively minnow and cast toward shore. I remember thinking, "Well, if the big bass won't hit, maybe I can salvage the day with a couple little ones."

The next hour was unforgettable. Not for the brilliant sunset that sealed the day, nor even for the piercing wails of a loon from far across the lake. The first cast netted a three-quarter-pound black crappie and within twenty minutes, a limit catch of fifteen crappie was thrashing noisily in the live well. None were large, but each put up a respectable fight and each was as unexpected as the one before.

This incident and others similar to it have convinced me that the crappie is a fish for *all* seasons. Catching "specs" may not be as easy in summer and fall as during the spring when fish are concentrated and convenient, but for the summer angler who knows "where, when and how to," the rewards are many.

When water temperatures have surpassed the seventy-degree mark, crappie are usually on the move to deep, cool waters of lakes and reservoirs. There they gather in massive schools (usually according to size) in waters as deep as thirty-five feet, but most often within the ten- to twenty-five-foot range. In these depths, however, crappie move either up or down during the day to feed or simply to loaf in layers of well-oxygenated, cool water.

Fishing in the shallows is generally a waste of time during the hot summer months, though crappie may move into shallower water—from five to fifteen feet—during early morning or late afternoon. Otherwise, crappie can be found congregating around deep underwater structures.

What is a structure? This is an all-inclusive term for those objects we have been fishing over and around for the past century. A structure may be a brush pile, rocky

Texan works a brush pile for crappie.

reef, well-defined sandbar, drop-off, or any natural or artificially-created change in the bottom contour.

The crappie, like largemouth bass and other popular sport fish, spend nearly every moment of its life on or near structures.

The summer crappie angler now becomes more of a hunter. The challenge is to find these structures where large schools of crappie gather for food and cover. This task is often difficult, but can be made considerably easier with the aid of a depth finder.

Armed with an electronic device, the angler can "read" the bottom contour for abrupt changes in depth. "Blips" or bright flashes on

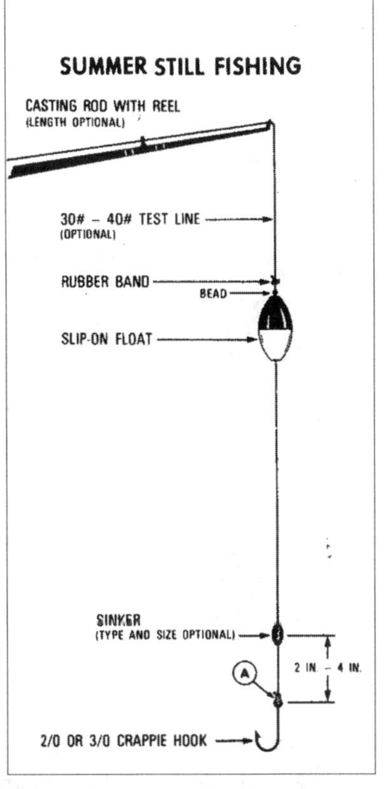

the scanner suggest rock or brush piles, old creek channels, roads, or submerged timber. But let's assume we don't have a depth finder. Can we still locate crappie?

In the summer, the angler must search out the crappie's chosen water level where large schools of fish are strung out horizontally within the thin layer of water that provides their "comfort temperature." Fishing a foot above or below these schools may not produce fish. You have to be "right on."

Start your fishing in a sheltered bay, cove or along a weed line in water from fifteen to twenty-five feet. Depth may be determined by lowering a cord with a lead weight or a one ounce bell sinker attached. (The cord should be pre-measured and marked at five-foot intervals.)

Next, lower a small, lively minnow—hooked through the lips or back—to the bottom. If no strike results, raise the bait two or three

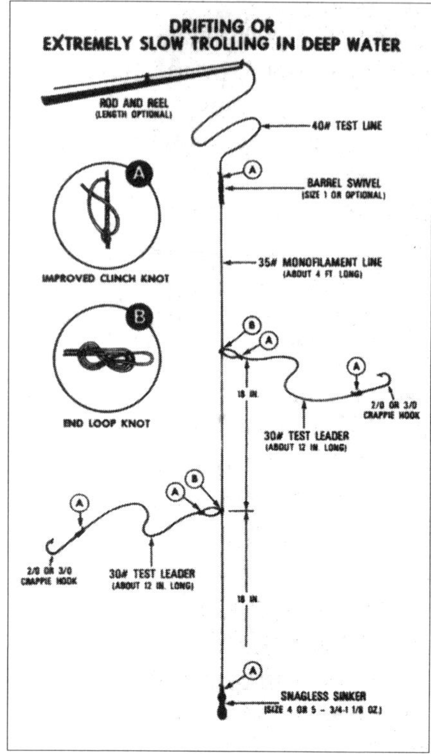

feet, and again, allow the bait to work while occasionally twitching the rod tip.

Continue this procedure until the bait reaches the surface. After three or four attempts, if no crappie has struck, move to another promising spot and try again.

If still-fishing produced nothing, switch to drifting or trolling. Drift fishing is probably the best technique for catching lunker crappie. Wind speeds measuring from five to fifteen miles per hour, quite common in summer and fall, will push the average boat along at a speed which is perfect for deep-running crappie lures.

When wind conditions are not right, either velocity or direction, trolling can be productive. This is best accomplished with a smaller outboard or electric motor. Crappie strike best at slow-moving lures, so you may have to troll in reverse in order to maintain a slower boat speed.

Trolling is most productive toward morning or evening. Work slowly along the shore, particularly around rocky points, weed beds, trees hanging over the water, the ends of boat docks or edges of drop-offs.

Once a school of crappie is found, mark the spot so you can either anchor just outside the school and cast into it, or continue to troll or drift around the concentration. You can use a store-bought marker buoy or make your own.

Anything will do, including white bleach jugs, over-sized bobbers, pieces of Styrofoam or any floatable item (the exceptions being, of course, glass bottles or jars.) Attach to a length of cord with a heavy bell sinker or lead weight.

You can take crappie from one of these marked spots for several hours, unless the fish are spooked away. And this brings up a matter of fishing ethics. Several times I have watched fishermen move in on another angler's marker, and soon the air is filled with cussing and name-calling, thus turning a pleasurable outing into a bitter memory.

Respect another fisherman's marker and fish only on the perimeter of the marked area. However, the angler with the marker should also be considerate enough to realize that, on a public lake, a marker is not like staking claim to a gold mine.

Now—let's get back to fishing. When trolling or drifting, different lures and fishing rigs must be employed than those used during spring when fish are in the shallows. There are many ingenious deep water rigs that have originated in various states. The type of rig, however, may be determined by existing state fishing laws that regulate the number of hooks or baits per line.

Minnesota, for example, allows the angler one fishing pole—except in winter when two are permissible—with one line and one hook on its inland waters. But in some states, anglers may use multiple hook and line combinations. The most popular rig for deep water trolling or drifting is a single spinner, fly or jig baited with a minnow and a heavy split shot for weight.

A common setup in brushy or snag-filled areas is a #4 or #5 snagless sinker tied to the end of a line and, above that, one or several twelve-inch, thirty-pound test leaders with #2/0 or #3/0 crappie hooks, (see illustration on page 72.)

In many states crappie anglers use a light-weight, plastic T-bar from which three to as many as nine droplines extend. Each line is baited with a minnow, and occasionally a fisherman may catch two or more crappies at a time.

In Georgia, an old fishing buddy showed me a T-bar made of metal which acted as a sinker. But in this case a small float was at-

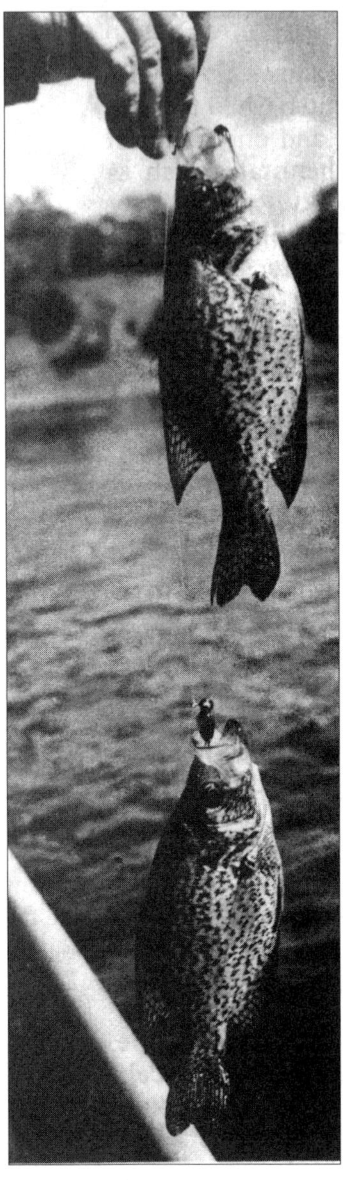

A double!

tached to the base of the T. Several lines baited with minnows were then tied to the crossbar in the T.

Other anglers may use an L-shaped wire attachment or a Y-swivel (see illustration on page 70). Attach a nylon leader about three feet long to your line and on the other end of the leader, add a heavy weight (about an ounce.) Tie a Y-swivel (also called three-way swivel) ten inches up from the sinker to a monofilament extension about eight inches in length. Tie a hook to this. Go up the leader about fifteen inches and tie another Y-swivel to another extension and hook. The Y-swivel eliminates any chance of the lines fouling.

I remember another angling entrepreneur in southern Wisconsin who claimed he couldn't decide whether his first fishing love was crappie or walleye. And so, he would troll with a deep-running walleye lure and about thirty inches above that, he added a length (about two feet) of six-pound monofilament line to which he had tied a plastic beetle and a live minnow. Apparently he knew what he was doing, for he proudly displayed a "mixed bag" of both crappie and walleye.

Even the best crappie rig won't produce unless it is pulling the right bait or lure. During summer, successful anglers rely heavily on live bait such as minnows or worms on small, long-shanked hooks. However, many deep-running artificials can be deadly, including spinner-fly combos, small crankbaits, beetle-type lures, two- or three-inch plastic worms and small Maribou jigs.

My personal favorite is the small one-sixteenth-ounce bee-type jig, tied in either black and yellow or red and black chenille and tipped with a two-inch minnow. To improve my success, a single spinner blade, especially one which revolves slowly when trolled, can be at-tached to almost any artificial lure.

Summer fishing for crappie should be predicated on two major factors, wind and light. Fish do not have eyelids or irises to shut out or reduce the amount of light striking their eyes. Light penetration is not a problem in spring when the sun's rays strike the water at an oblique angle. But in summer, as the sun moves higher in the sky, light penetration increases. Thus, crappie are forced to find shade around structures or by moving deeper.

The angler should plan accordingly. On cloudy, cool days crappie usually will not school as deep and probably will be scattered over many different areas. On warm sunny days they will school more tightly in deeper water or in areas providing optimum shade such as under docks, in weed beds or brush piles, or even inside hollow stumps.

Wind is vitally important in the summer. With the right wind speed and direction, the angler can drift slowly over old underwater channels, along sheer drop offs, flooded forests, and other structures.

When the wind is either too gusty or non-existent, the angler should move into the sheltered bays and weed patches.

As a general rule, a little ripple of wind on the surface will not adversely affect your success. But as wind and waves increase, crappie fishing success will decrease. Another rule to follow: during early morning or late afternoon, if winds increase, so should the depth at which you fish.

There are, of course, exceptions to all these widely-accepted rules of crappie fishing. Accordingly, we should remember another impor-tant exception to one of the most commonly-accepted axioms in the world of fishing—that slabbies are too difficult to find and catch after spring spawning is over. Nothing could be further from the truth!

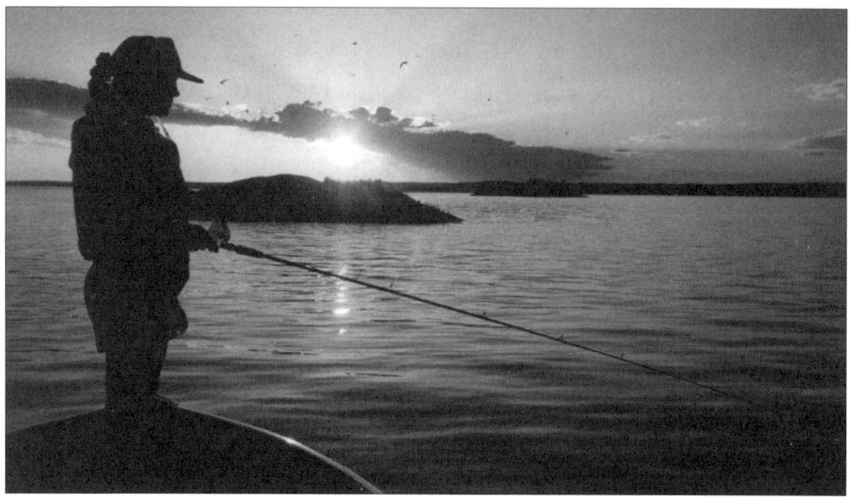

Chapter Ten
"Brushing Up" on Crappie

Brush piles and dead timber make good crappie cover.

The brush pile is one of the most important structures for locating both black and white crappies, regardless of the time of day, season of the year, or type of water.

The brush pile provides all of life's basic necessities for crappie. It is a veritable underwater cafeteria in addition to being a source of shade and protection. Within a few days or weeks after a brush pile is introduced into a body of water, myriad small aquatic organisms begin to gather in and around the complex maze of branches and twigs. Shortly, small bait fish and minnows discover these minute organisms and these, in turn, are discovered by crappie.

If you have pinpointed some of these underwater structures you probably will enjoy angling success. But for those who have not located a brush pile, why not make one of your own?

Many ardent crappie fishermen construct and place their own brush piles. They consistently outfish other anglers. They anchor over a brush pile or fish the structure from shore. If the spot is unproductive, they move on to the next site and so on. Over some brush piles they catch five or six crappie, while others yield none. At the end of an average day, however, their take is generally very good.

Fish shelters in particular help fishing success in early spring and late fall when natural vegetative cover is lacking in lakes and streams. However, the brush pile is even more important on reservoirs because many of these man-made lakes have very little bottom-growing vegetation.

So, how do you prepare a brush pile? It's easy. First, find desirable-sized trees, four to eight feet in height that are very bushy. Cedars, willows, and especially spent Christmas trees work well.

Next, tie a heavy rock to the tree base so it will be held in a relatively vertical position underwater. Anchored this way, the tree is less likely to claim a lot of tackle since the hooks can usually be worked up the ascending limbs.

If several trees are used, they should be tied together with twine, weighted with rocks and sunk. It should be stated here that state laws vary regarding sinking anything in the water, so check first.

The proper depth for placing your brush pile will vary, of course, depending on whether your favorite fishing hole is a reservoir, natural lake or river. In reservoirs, the structure should be located close enough to the shore so it can be fished with a cane pole. The pile should be placed anytime from November through March when water levels are generally down. When high water returns around April or May, the pile should lie in eight to ten feet of water.

In northern states in the past, anglers have bundled the brush pile on shore during winter and tow the structure out onto the ice. In spring the ice melts and the brush pile sinks to the bottom, usually in from ten to fifteen feet of water.

Investigations by fishery researchers have shown that shelters about six feet high provide the best fishing (assuming that the brush pile is sunk in ten feet of water). Brush piles located from four to six feet below the surface are at a perfect depth for easy fishing by almost any method.

Rivers are another matter. Crappies generally congregate in shallower water and thus the brush pile should be low, flat and sunk in six to eight feet.

Where should you sink a brush pile? If you are not familiar with a body of water, ask at local bait or tackle shops. Merchants are usually happy to give directions to productive areas. Check also with local game wardens or conservation officers for any laws regulating the depositing of brush piles, and if legal, where to sink them.

On natural lakes and rivers in many states, existing statutes restrict the placement of trees, branches and other previously-mentioned items in public waters. Again, be sure to review pertinent state laws before placing your brush pile.

To find a good place for your brush, scout out brushy coves or points having water depths from ten to twenty feet. Lake maps that show bottom contours can be of great aid in locating likely areas such as near drop-offs, ditches, and creek channels.

When placing brush piles or "stake beds" be sure to tote along a lake map. Mark each specific site on your map. Do not use a buoy to mark the spot, but select several landmarks to enable you to find the exact spot without difficulty. Permanent buoys can get entwined in props of outboard motors or they might be struck by water skiers. With this in mind, do not locate your brush pile where it might create a hazard for swimmers, boaters, or other fishermen trolling or drift-fishing for pike.

In several states, placing of large brush piles by fishery crews have been a boon to crappie angling. These huge "mats" as they are called consist of trees, limbs, logs, or brush wired together and sunk with stones to the lake bottom. A good mat will cover several hundred square feet and be at least four to five feet high.

Is constructing and placing a brush pile worth all the time and effort? Let these facts be your answer. Catch rates for anglers using experimental stake beds on several Tennessee reservoirs were three to five times greater than lakewide averages. Years ago a man-made brush pile in a lake in Illinois produced more than 20,000 crappie in a single season. Still have any doubt?

Chapter Eleven

Fly Fishing for Crappie

For years the fly rod and reel were used only by trout fishermen. But recently, countless anglers have discovered the charm and excitement in panfishing with a fly rod.

Fly fishing is unlike any other type of angling. But don't let anyone tell you it is a technique too difficult to master—that's hogwash! No doubt, fly fishing does require some finesse but with a bit of coordination and some practice, you will soon master the art.

Of course many anglers have avoided the fly rod because they were somehow led to believe that fly fishing equipment costs too much money. More nonsense! Fly rodding can be done as cheaply or as lavishly as you want to make it.

Here is all the crappie angler needs to get started. First, you will need a seven- to eight-foot graphite fly rod weighing about four or five ounces. It needs to be flexible, yet stout enough to enable you to cast forty feet of line.

Next you will need a fly reel. The primary function of the reel is simply to store line, not to help fight the fish as in spinning outfits. You can choose from several models of automatic or single-action fly reels. But the beginner can easily get by with an inexpensive, single-action reel with a click device instead of a drag.

Fly lines come in various profiles or configurations of outside diameters. Use any double-taper line suitable for casting dry flys, small streamers, and poppers. Recommended is a heavier, weight-forward line, preferably white in color so it is easier to watch.

The leader should be the tapered type, stiff in the butt section and fine toward the tip. A six-pound monofilament tip works fine for crappie.

And there you have it—a well-balanced fishing outfit that should not cost more than fifty-five dollars.

Learning to fly cast is not difficult but it will require reading up on it or firsthand instruction and some practice. Fly casting techniques are taught in some adult-education programs or at numerous live demonstrations, seminars, and clinics

Such techniques as the roll cast, double-haul cast, side cast, and left and right loops can best be learned from personal instruction. But, to help you learn there are a number of books and brochures available from tackle shops and sporting goods outlets.

The objective to fly fishing is to cast a heavy line that takes out a light lure. This is opposite of spin casting, where a heavy lure pulls the line out over the water.

However, you do not always have to cast to catch crappie. Most anglers use fly rods to work brush piles from shore or from a boat by simply dabbling a small jig or minnow. This technique, called "dunking," is used around bushy areas, where casting would leave you constantly snagged with tree limbs and branches. Here, the trick is to drop the bait down through the maze of branches or root systems. Once your lure penetrates the maze, it's usually just a matter of time before a fish hits.

Fly rod aficionados in different parts of the country have their favorite lures and methods for catching crappie. In Florida, many anglers cast puffy white dry flies amidst the thick blanket of lily pads in mangrove swamps.

Probably the favorite among most throughout the United States is a one-sixty-fourth- or one-thirty-second-ounce pink or white hair jig, attached to a seven-foot tapered leader and a white fly line.

Casting weighted jigs, however, is a more difficult technique for the beginner to master. Briefly, here are a few things to remember. First, the casting motion must be slower than normal to allow the small weighted jig to move through the air. Unlike a dry fly, the lead head has weight, and thus slows down the fly line on the inward and outward thrusts.

The jig caster employs more arm and body motion than the fly caster, who relies primarily on forearm movement and wrist action. Point the rod at an angle (about forty-five degrees) away from your body. This eliminates any chance of the jig hitting the back of your head on the forward motion!

Retrieve the jig slowly and deliberately. Always keep the rod tip low and work the lure back with long but jerky pulls. Speed up through each pull, but just before completing the pull, ease up. Often strikes occur at this point.

Most important in fly rod fishing is to watch the line carefully. Sometimes the only indication of a strike will be a slight twitch or bounce in your line.

The mouth of a crappie is not as sensitive as that of bass and carp. Thus a crappie will usually not reject an artificial lure for several seconds. So, instead of the telltale twitch, the angler may see the line moving backward or to one side or another. This is your indication to set the hook—immediately!

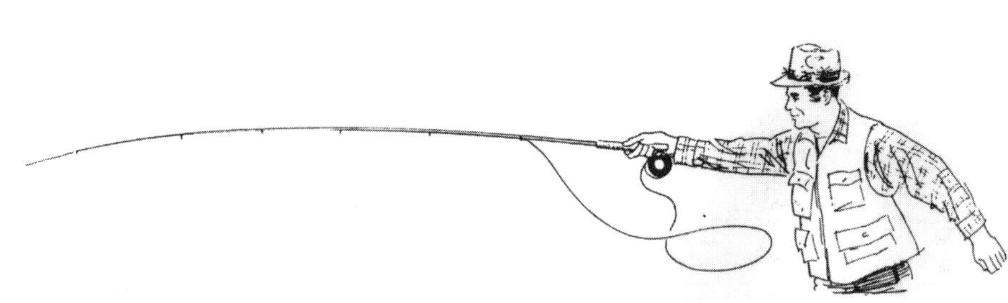

The fly rod's length gives the angler excellent leverage. Thus, a simple upward thrust of the arm will set the hook in a crappie's tender mouth. As in any fishing, once the hook is set, a tight line must be maintained or the hook will fall out.

In addition to many other types of lures, flys and live baits will produce good results. Two other favorites for crappie are popping flys and nymphets. Poppers may be made of cork, balsa, or plastic foam. Best colors are green, yellow, and black or any combinations of the three colors. Best sizes are #10, #12, and #14.

Popping for crappie is especially exciting because the strike can be seen. Present the bug in an appropriate spot, and then jerk the lure back with short, nervous twitches. Each twitch will cause the lure to "pop" on the surface. Pop the lure once, twice, or even three times in quick succession. Then allow it to rest for a second or two and resume the retrieve.

Different fish strike lures in many different ways. Probably the most unusual feeding procedure I have witnessed was by a ravenous school of crappie on an Indiana lake. Working a popper over a placid

surface toward evening, I saw a large crappie catapult into the air and back into the water with a noisy splash.

Thinking he had taken my lure, I immediately jerked the popper which came rocketing back, narrowly missing my head. This comical situation was repeated four or five more times. A fish would leap, and I would set hook, but each time—no fish!

Totally confused, I settled back onto the boat seat to mull over my predicament. I just noticed a mayfly on the water a scant six feet from the boat. Suddenly a crappie leapt directly over the insect and arched downward with its wide-opened mouth landing smack-dab on the fly. Once again, nature had taught me a fishing lesson.

The very next cast another crappie leapt near my popper, but this time I let the little bug sit. Sure enough, the fish inhaled the lure on his downward flight and soon my first slabbie lay on the floor of the boat to be joined by a dozen more before the day ended.

Late spring and summer are my favorite times for nymphet fishing. The nymphet derives its name from two basic flys—the "nymph" or immature stage of an insect, and the "wet fly," when the adult fly dies, sinks or is washed under the surface. The nymphet use a combination of these two flys, both of which represent the life cycles of an insect occurring below the water surface.

Generally, crappies are minnow feeders, but on lakes and rivers where young crappie feed heavily on flies and aquatic invertebrates, the nymphet can be extremely effective. On one such lake in north central Minnesota, a fishing buddy lays claim to a piscatorial lode. With fly rod and nymphets, he catches upwards of 600 crappie a summer.

Using an eight-foot fly rod and a #8 nymphet in brown or green, he works the weedy bays of his lake in depths from fifteen to twenty feet. After the lure hits the water, he counts to five or six, which allows the weighted lure to sink to depths from five to eight feet. Exactly when he starts the retrieve is determined by the depth where crappie seem to be resting.

He retrieves the lure, pausing briefly between long, three-foot pulls. He claims the lure works madness on crappie. Most of the fish run small, however, and he returns nearly all of them except enough for an occasional meal.

There are many fly casters who refuse to use any of the new poppers and jig-type lures. These ardent fly rod specialists use white or yellow streamers in either feather or marabou, usually in sizes #4 or #6. The streamers represent a minnow darting erratically through the water. Once again a slow retrieve is essential, though the streamer should never be allowed to remain motionless. A slow, darting action can be accomplished using short, ten-inch pulls on the fly line.

Crappie will also rise to dry flies. As in trout fishing, the crappie angler must present a fly similar in color, style, and size to the type of insect hatching on a lake at any given time.

Sometime it can be difficult matching the fly with nature's foods. I remember a quiet evening on a Missouri lake where a steady shower of cottonwood seeds drifted down onto the surface. I watched for nearly an hour as crappies fed hungrily on the seeds. Naturally I had no lure to imitate these seeds and I went home skunked.

The important part of dry-fly fishing is the presentation. The fly must be dropped as quietly and as close as possible to a school of feeding

When crappie turn finicky and ignore artificials, smart anglers switch to live baits—worms and nightcrawlers, grasshoppers, crickets, and even corn.

crappie. Once that is accomplished, forget about any retrieve. Just let it set—the fish should come to you.

In the fall, many anglers switch to live baits for calicoes. Crickets, katydids, and grasshoppers are excellent, as are angleworms and nightcrawlers. But you have to catch your bait before you can catch crappie.

Look for crickets under rocks, stones, or brick structures such as old walls or foundations. Grasshoppers can be collected in almost any open grassy field. Katydids can be found around porch lights in evening or on the lower branches of trees and shrubs. Any garden should have a bountiful supply of angleworms.

When using these small critters for bait, attach a bobber to your line for added casting weight. The #10 or #12 hooks work best, especially with the small insects.

Minnows can also be cast with a fly rod. But when casting a minnow or live insect, be sure to use a lob-type cast. This entails a much slower casting motion. The rod should be positioned at your side and the motion of your fly rod should be more circular than backward and forwards. This slow casting technique prevents the bait from being jerked off the hook.

Now that we've discussed some of the popular rod lures and techniques, how do we know where and when to use them? Unfortunately, most fly casting is done in relatively shallow water, about ten feet or less. The exceptions are streamers and nymphets, which can be fished in deeper water. Thus, you will have to schedule your fly rod fishing to those periods when fish have moved into shallower waters either to spawn or to feed.

The best time of day for crappie is early morning or late afternoon when winds usually have subsided and crappie are feeding in and around weed beds, stumps, lily pads, and boat docks. Look for surface swirls of feeding fish or any numerous small V's cut through the water surface. These are caused by small minnows or bait fish fleeing larger predators such as crappie.

Success in fly casting depends a great deal on the accuracy of your casts. The angler that drops a popper or a fly in the wake of a swirling crappie is certain to catch fish.

All this sounds difficult? I hope not. The fly rod can open a new frontier in your world of fishing. Basic equipment is not expensive and requires less maintenance and repair than spinning tackle. And the beauty of the fly rod is that even small crappie seem like fierce fighters with a flexible, sensitive fly rod bouncing in your hands.

Fly casters take great pride in their sport. But most are not the snobs sometimes assumed. To him or her, there is just as much pure joy in laying out a smooth cast as there is in fighting a burly game fish. Fly rodding is just another way to have fishing fun.

Don't miss fishing downstream below wasked out dams and old roadway pilings for your favorite panfish.

A Super Panfish Fly—The Muddler

Created on the Nipigon River, in Ontario's wilderness by my father, Don Gapen, in 1936 for brook trout, the Muddler is devastating on all game fish. the angler needs only to change the size of a Muddler minnow to see it work on his favorite fish. Changing the size and presentation gives the user the ability to cause the Muddler to represent insect life, nymph life, minnows, or a dry fly's appearance.

Though the original use was to represent the soulpin minnow so prevelant in the fast, rocky waters of the Nipigon, when scaled down to size #14 and #12, it imitates a great insect or floating fly for bluegill. when forced ti sink, a #6 or #8 successfully mimickes a minnow to entice crappie.

Do to the Muddler's buoyant deer-hair construction, it does well when insect life flounders across quiet evening lake surfaces.

A Tip: To effectively sink the buoyant Muddler fly, place it in your mouth, soak it with saliva, then crush the air out of its hollow deer-hair head. On your next cast, it will immediately sink to represent a emerging nymph larva, a drowned dry fly, or a crippled fish fry.

If left in its buoyant floating stage, the Muddler can be "popped" along the surface like a small panfish popper. Add a little dry fly float material and see this fly continue to hold its buoyancy for an hour or so.

When the chips are down and panfishing is touch and go, I always switch to the original Muddler fly, a gift my father left fishing world.

Dan Gapen, Sr.

Dan Gapen, Sr., with a decent crappie caught on his father's fly, the Muddler Minnow.

Chapter Twelve

Lake Okeechobee:
A Panfish Paradise

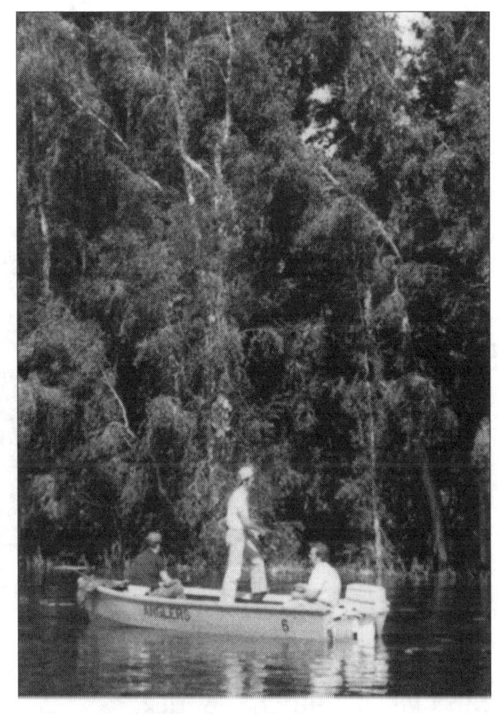

Mention Okeechobee, and the bass pro will conjure up images of ten-pound bass. Yup, the huge round lake situated in the southern tip of Florida between Little and Big Cypress swamps is famous for largemouth bass. Maybe so, but when I hear the word "Okeechobee" I visualize stringers or live wells of heavy panfish, especially bluegill, or bream, as the natives of southern Florida call them.

Years ago when my dear friend Dave Conn and I were fishing Dick Vance's fish camp out of Clewiston, Florida, we stumbled across a side channel loaded with surface-sucking bluegill. When confronting our host, he admitted the backwaters and canals were loaded with panfish, so many that bream were considered pests by the local fraternity.

Ten-pound bass fishing had been slow, and it didn't take a lot of thought to divert our minds to giving these local "pests" a try.

"Crickets are the only bait those useless fish will take. You can get a hundred live crickets and a cricket cage down at Henry's Bait Shop on Main Street," Vance announced as Dave and I told him of our plan.

We'd buy crickets, that was a for sure, but I'd thought I'd also like to try a few Yankee methods on them with my Father's Muddler Fly and a fly rod. A three-fourths-ounce weight, seven-and-one-half-

foot rod loaded with a seven-and-one-half-foot mono leader and a #10 Muddler should do the trick.

My buddy Dave would use one of our "Slip-n-Lock" floats with a small one-thirty-second-ounce black or brown Ugly Bug jig on a five-and-one-half-foot ultra lite spinning rod.

Because we were able to visibly see the darting panfish in the one to one and one-half feet of channel edge waters, the float and Ugly Bug were locked in a position where only ten inches separated float and jig.

Disgusted with our decision to go after the fish locals called pests, Dick decided to stay home. We were on our own!

It took us only five minutes to motor up the lake's main border channel to reach the first off-shoot that meandered between the main lake and the channel. Another twenty yards into the narrow, shallow inlet produced the first sighting of panfish. The entire inlet, which snaked its way hundreds of feet towards the main lake, was closed over near the cypress tree tops by a heavy vine cover. This left our target structure completely in shadow.

As we eased our way inward, several schools of panfish, which turned out to be bream, flushed out of the shallows on either bank.

Taking this as our cue to begin casting, Dave led off with his spinning gear. No sooner did his bobber settle than a half-pound bream engaged the tiny Ugly Bug.

"Dan, on this light rod and the four-pound line, this fish is putting up a good fight," my partner commented as he lifted the sparky fish aboard.

My first cast to the opposite side ended in a similar result. The floating #10 Muddler was struck instantly after it was twitched a second time on surface. No need for live crickets this day.

At the time there was a limit of fifty bluegill per person on Okeechobee. Dave and I had managed to harvest half a limit in the next hundred yards. All the ones we kept to eat were in excess of a half pound with the top fish slightly over a pound. Ten-pound bass be darned, these Okeechobee bluegill were a treat I wouldn't have passed up.

During the next two days, morning bass fishing continued to be slow with our largest bass a bit over eight pounds. It had taken a live shiner.

We finally convinced Dick, our host, at the Clewiston Motel and Resort to come with us on the second noon outing for panfish. Not

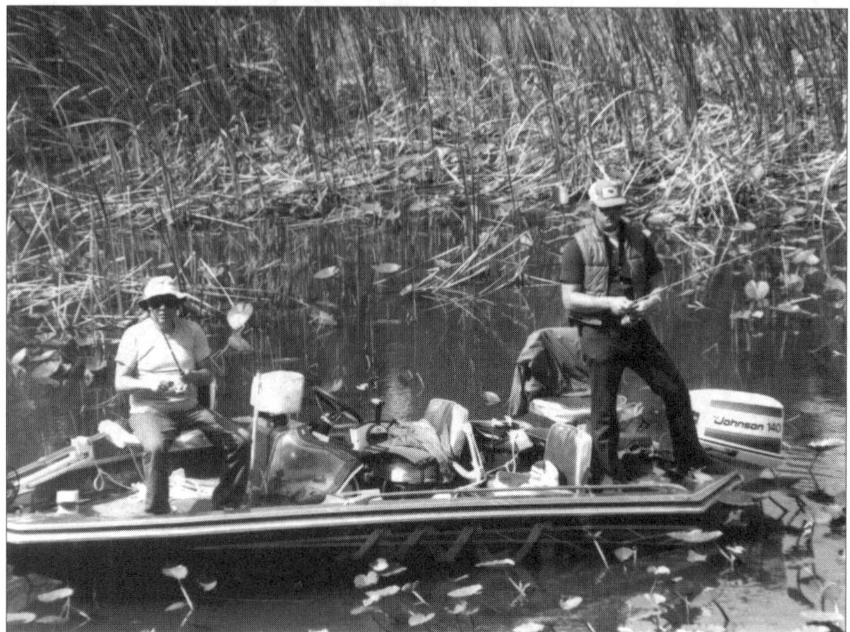

Dave Conn and Dick Vance search out bream.

that this bass man would ever acknowledge it, but I believed he enjoyed those rather fat bream of the Okeechobee backwater canals.

Further explaining the sawgrass and lily pad structures of Okeechobee Lake saw us find a goodly amount of crappie and a different bluegill species that locals call stump knockers. Old Ben Smurd had shown me stump knockers a year before in an erie dark swamp in southern Georgia so the blunt-nosed panfish wasn't new to me. However, the ones we caught in the roots of the cypress trees were larger and a whole lot darker.

Day in and day out if you were to ask me what was the best bluegill (bream or stumpknocker) lake I'd ever fished, I'd have to say Okeechobee Lake near Clewiston, Florida.

If you ever decide to fish Okeechobee for trophy bass, don't forget to take your panfish gear along. And, don't forget to get a cage full of crickets from Henry's Bait Shop—not that you'll need them, but it's "tradition" you know.

As far as crappie fishing goes, the main canal circling the main lake will probably produce all you'll want. If you're a serious crappie angler, try working the shallow north half of the lake. It seems this is where all the die hard calico bream anglers (crappie name by locals) spend their time fishing. Another name the locals use on crappie is the "silver perch." In the north there seems to be a lot more brush and flooded dead timber, natural habitat for the calicoes.

But I must admit, when you can harvest overly fat, one-pound bluegill, which fight like hell, why bother with one-pound slim crappie which put up little fight and fillet harder.

It's your choice!

Boat positioned for bedding for crappie.

Chapter Thirteen

Ol' Google-eyes & Distant Cousin Mojarra

Mention the word goggle-eye to any Indiana stream angler and their eyes will light up. My dear friend Bayou Bill Scifres, a writer for the Indianapolis newspapers and *Outdoor Life* magazine loved to fish this fellow.

The goggle-eye, better known as a rock bass, can be found throughout most of the central states and many of the provinces of Canada. Because ol' goggle-eye is a crawdad feeder, he's easily taken on nightcrawlers, garden worms, or any artificial lure which takes on the appearance of a crawfish. One of the best is an orange-and-brown one-eighth-ounce Ugly Bug tipped with an inch or so of crawler. Here you have the appearance and smell of a crawfish. Acidity in a worm is almost exactly the same as found in a crawfish.

Late one hot July day years ago, I was treated to a lesson on rock bass fishing by Bayou Bill I'll never forget. We'd fish Paw-Paw Creek, a tiny stream no wider than ten feet near his home.

Equipment for the day would be an old pair of sneakers, tattered blue jeans, a can of worms, several one-sixteenth-ounce Ugly Bugs, a six-foot light spinning outfit and a wide-brimmed straw hat to shade us from the sun. We'd wade upstream from old County Road 24 to the next wooden bridge crossing, a matter of half a mile.

"Dan, we won't bother fishing the straight stretches, they're too shallow. We'll take turns dabbling the holes on the spots where the creek turns," came my instructions as we began our assault on Paw-Paw.

Bill would take the first hole as I took in the lesson I was about to learn. As we approached the first bend, Bill took the lead and quietly slipped up to the downstream branch of an old cottonwood which now rested in the creek. Leaning across the snag, he dropped his crawler-loaded Ugly Bug into a slow eddy which swirled downstream from the fallen tree's main trunk.

"There's a hole created by this trunk where I've always found goggle-eyes. And if there's one there, there'll be more," Bill commented as the first big-eyed round-bodied fish sucked in the offering.

Swinging the first fish to hand, Ol' Bill said this could just be the beginning. By the gleeful grin on his face, I had no doubt more would follow. I was asked to join him.

Gently I took a position next to my buddy, who now stood butt deep in water. Bill had been dragging an old cloth sack into which he now dumped the flopping half-pound fish.

"This one stays with us for a fish and hush puppy supper, Dan," came Bill's exclamation as I gave him a strange look. Where I come from all the bass and walleye pros had always said rock bass were full of worms during hot weather. When asked, my buddy scoffed at the idea. "Sweetest meat you'll ever eat," was his response to my suggestion.

By now we both dropped our worm-tipped jigs back into the holes. Instantly as they settled into the four-foot holes, they were hit. My light six-foot rod jerked down hard as I set the hook. This fish had some character and after a couple strong pulsating circles ol' goggle-eyes thrashed to surface. This one would weigh nearly a pound. Bayou Bill yelped, "Good-un," as he also set hook into another fish. His turned out to be a half-pound smallmouth that he released while admiring the bigger than hand-sized fish I'd just landed.

"My God, Dan, that's a dandy! She'll eat great! Put her in here in my flour sack," my companion instructed as he opened the fish stringer line at the top of the sack which now trailed downstream from his waist.

After four more fish, the hole quieted, and we moved upstream, never walking the bank, always in the creek channel.

I know from years of trout fishing that when you fish rivers, walking upstream gives you the best chance of quietly approaching your prey. Such an approach sees all the disturbance you create by your wading approach travel away downstream from you as you work to the upstream-holding fish.

"Bobber" Anne with a rock bass that fell prey to a red-and-white Flub-Dub plug.

Rock bass are a school fish by nature. Where you find one, there will be others. Spawning occurs in late spring when water temperatures reach sixty-five degrees. The female will lay from 4,000 to 10,000 eggs, laid in a bed similar to that of other panfish where the adhesive eggs stick to the gravel and stone base of the bed. Eggs will hatch in three to four days depending on the water temperature. The male will guard the nest, while growth of the hatching young is rapid. During their first year rock bass go from an egg to as much as three inches in length. Survival out of a hatch of 4,000 eggs that first year can be as many as 500. Throughout their life, they are a target food of other species such as largemouth bass, northern pike, and muskie.

Bill and I worked our way up to the Paw-Paw's next bend and, as he'd told me, we found another productive hole. Once again, "dabbling," a form of vertical jigging with the Ugly Bug did the trick.

After three hours, we'd reached hole number six. The flour sack was a third full—more than enough fillets for a decent supper.

Bayou Bill, my dear friend, taught me one other lesson about rock bass. They love leeches! Being that Gapen's was the first to design a jig and worm combo called the Hairy Worm, Bill was a steadfast believer in a one-sixteenth-ounce black Hairy Worm. He made it famous in Indiana with his outdoor column in the Indianapolis papers. Before I introduced my friend to the Ugly Bug, he wouldn't venture out on a local stream without a handful of Hairy Worms. As well as we were doing that day, by the time we'd reached the third hold, he'd switched. I didn't believe it worked any better than my favorite Ugly Bug, but Bill pointed out that it wasn't necessary to tip the Hairy Worm with a piece of worm to achieve similar results. He was right!

Now the Mojarra
Or as it is called in Texas, the Rio Grande perch.

Rio Grande perch, the mojarra.

My introduction to mojarra fishing came when my dear old buddy Dave Conn and I went to Lake Guerrero in Mexico. I'd never caught the hump-backed panfish up until then. Dave gave it the nickname "Peter perch," a name he'd conjured up one hot afternoon in

Guerrero when I asked for some red cherries to put in my soft drink. For years I wasn't one to drink alcohol, but in a bar I refused to call my ginger ale loaded with cherries a "Shirley Temple."

Thus, after Dave and I had done battle with several of the bull-dog-looking panfish my fishing partner decided to call the tough little guys "Peter perch"! I have no idea.

High noon and a siesta had come and gone on our first day when we first encountered a mojarra. Bass fishing had slowed and, at my suggestion, the guide took us into the pockets in the flooded thorn brush. Having been using a one-quarter-ounce Hairy Worm for bass, there wasn't any need to change lures. I surmised the open water bass might have retreated to the shade provided by these flooded trees. Was I ever wrong!

My first cast saw me hang on a thorn bush and here my Hairy Worm combo cut off. "Go to a one-eighth-ounce size, señor," suggested our guide, Henry. A lighter weight wouldn't snag as easily, were his thoughts. Done!

My next cast saw the Hairy Worm fall only six feet down the edge of the brush before being hit hard. The circling fight that followed reminded me of a large bluegill. And when my fish came to hand, it

A young Dan Gapen years ago with a Mexican mojarra.

Dave Corm, Dan's dear friend, with a stringer of mojarra kept for supper.

wasn't a bass but a beautifully colored panfish-like fish with a huge knot above its eyes.

"Mojarra," cried Henry, "Good to eat!"

Once in hand, Henry carefully palmed the fish and tossed it into the bucket beside him. It became obvious he'd been expecting to land a few of these colorful spiny panfish. Why else would the bucket be there?

Dave was next to hit this new fish. Instantly it made a hard run into the thorn bush structure it had been hiding near. A moment later Dave's line snapped, a victim of sharp thorns. That wouldn't be the last Ugly Bug we'd lose to the thorn bush and the mojarra. By the end of our trip, we were out of jigs and had gone to using twenty-pound mono for presenting our jigs. At least the heavier line enabled us to land three out of five fish hooked. An ultra light rod and reel loaded with twenty-pound line isn't the easiest gear to use, but it was a partial remedy to our loss of fish and lures.

That night at the resort our camp cook deep fried the mojarra fillets and served the golden-brown fish with a Mexican version of hush puppies. We'd insist on a similar meal a couple more times before our week-long fishing trip to Guerrero ended. Simply put they were delicious!

The mojarra appears to be part of the panfish family but is only found in the Caribbean Islands, northern South America, and Central America. Only found in waters in the United States that border with north Mexico, this fish has been given the name "Rio Grande perch" in Texas. It is one member of the fish family called Gerreidae. All school-like panfish take on the panfish characteristics and look similar to the species we call sunfishes. Unlike crappie, this fish is a hard striker and a strong fighter. The one characteristic that sets the mojarra aside from the other sunfishes is the enormous lump directly above its eyes. This is a characteristic of the male of the species, while females have a more subdued hump. Where you find one, you'll probably find dozens more. In some areas, the mojarra has faint vertical bars on its sides under the numerous lime-dotted side plates.

Author's Note: *Both Bayou Bill and Dave Conn, the author's fishing buddies, have gone to another world where goggle-eye grow to ten pounds and ten-pound mojarra tear up any gear these two friends use on them.*

The author and these two old fishing buddies traveled extensively throughout North and South America, creating memories of a love for the sport of fishing which will last forever.

"I miss you terribly, guys!"

~ Dan Gapen, Sr.

Dave (left) fights hard to keep a fighting mojarra out of the brush. Mojarra, like other panfish love to hold in the flooded underwater tree limbs (above).

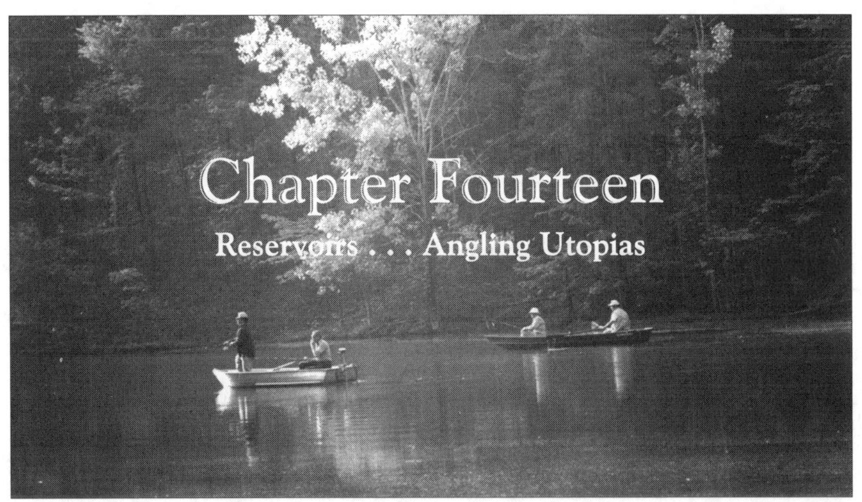

Chapter Fourteen
Reservoirs . . . Angling Utopias

About the turn of the century, there were 100 big reservoirs (over 500 acres) in the nation. Today, there are some 1,300 of them, encompassing about twelve million acres of water.

More than half of these impoundment waters are located in just a few states: Pennsylvania, Texas, South and North Carolina, Alabama, Montana, Tennessee, California, Oklahoma, Arkansas, and Kentucky. About half of the total water area in reservoirs is under direct control of the U.S. Corps of Engineers and the Bureau of Reclamation. The remainder is under private power and irrigation companies, state and municipal water supply, power and recreation agencies.

These vast man-made lakes have served as giant test tubes for fishery researchers and biologists. And, generally speaking, their experiments have been enormously successful. Outstanding sport fishing has been provided for black and white crappie, largemouth bass and many other fighting game fish.

A new reservoir is a fish manager's dream. They can select certain fish species that will readily adapt to their new habitat and multiply to tremendous numbers within an amazingly short span of time. Smith Mountain Reservoir in Virginia, for example, was stocked with largemouth bass. Within a handful of years the lake was overpopulated with ten- to eleven-inch bass. Anglers from all over came to catch the small fish and stories of anglers with 100 to 200 bass per boat became widespread.

Even today biologists are continuing to experiment with new fish species and management programs designed to provide quality angling. In several western states, for example, some reservoirs are being managed for "two-story" fishing. In the "upper story" fishermen can catch bass, crappie, and walleye; and in the "lower story," rainbow trout and other cold water fishes.

What the biologists haven't accomplished in our reservoirs, lady luck has. Virginia's Roanoke River was sealed off by a dam to form Kerr Reservoir. In the process, a number of ocean-dwelling striped bass that had moved up the river to spawn were trapped. Instead of perishing in their freshwater prison, they adapted to it readily. These huge fish have provided some great freshwater angling thrills in America.

But what about crappie? It is not an overstatement to say that reservoirs have increased crappie fishing a million times over. And without reservoirs, this book would be about one-tenth its size.

From Lake Zumbro in the hardwood-covered hills of southeastern Minnesota to sprawling Lake Texoma, an 85,000-acre impoundment on the Texas-Mexico border, crappie anglers are continuing to harvest a rich bounty of black and white crappie. These reservoirs are especially attractive to crappie anglers, for they offer liberal limits and an abundance of recreation facilities.

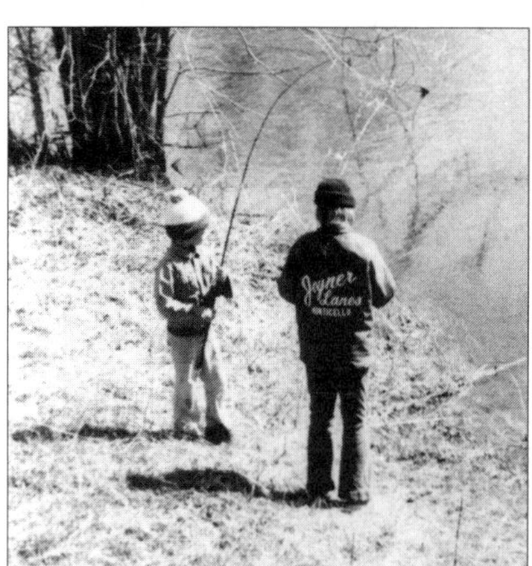
Buddies working the reservoir bank.

Texas angler ties into a spunky crappie amidst a flooded forest on Toledo Bend Lake.

To understand the fine points of crappie fishing on reservoir waters, the angler must first visualize how the land appeared before the impounded waters began to creep inexorably over the land.

After completing their initial surveys, watershed engineers know the exact water levels they wish to achieve throughout different areas of the watershed. Thus, forested areas that would be inundated are cleared of timber at least one year prior to the flooding process.

When trees and shrubs are cut, loggers usually leave a stump twelve to eighteen inches above ground. In that year before a forest is flooded, sprouting often occurs on the stump. Later, when the area is covered with water these sprouts provide natural habitat for crappie.

These spots, called stick-ups, may protrude above the surface for as long as ten years. The action of ice, wind, and waves, however, eventually break them off during low water levels in winter. With spring come higher water levels, and the stick-ups disappear beneath the surface. On reservoirs, stick-ups are prime gathering spots for crappie, and the angler who can locate them will usually have little difficulty filling their fish basket.

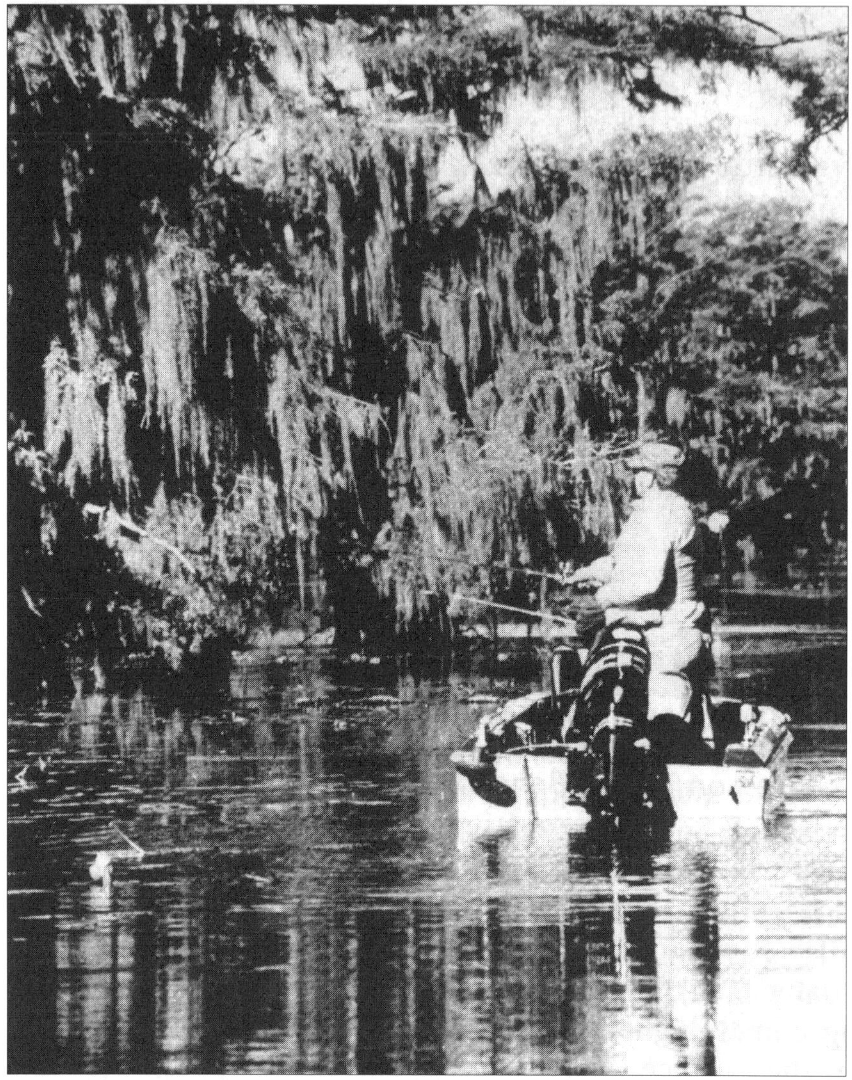

Spanish moss drapes heavily over flooded trees to form a picturesque setting for Texas crappie fishermen on Caddo Lake.

Trees that are not harvested prior to impounding usually break off several years after the flood waters lap over the land. These and their root systems also are gathering places for crappie.

The late Gim Dossett, director of Boat Docks and Camping Areas for the Kentucky Department of Parks, was probably the nation's most knowledgeable stump fisherman. Gim knew of one stump on the bottom of Kentucky Lake that was especially dear to him.

"There are literally thousands of stumps on the bottom of Kentucky Lake, and I've caught crappie around every one of 'em," boasted Gim. "But there is one down there that is something special."

"Before the area was flooded, I musta killed a hundred gray squirrels and even treed a few raccoons in the old white oak. But for the past twenty-seven years, the stump of that old oak has been the home for crappie and bass, not squirrels. There is no way I could count the number of fish I have taken from around that stump."

Just how long do these stumps last underwater? Gim also fished Reelfoot Lake in extreme western Kentucky and northwestern Tennessee. The lake was formed by the great earthquakes of 1811 and 1812, according to Gim, and it still has many tree stumps studding its bottom.

"My theory," explained Dossett, "is that as long as the air and insects can't get to 'em, stumps don't seem to rot or decay." Look at the trees after they're flooded. Once they die and have been exposed to the elements for about ten years, the top part rots away, but the portion under the water remains."

Anyway, a tip of the hat to Mother Nature for leaving us these stumps; for "stump jumping" is one of the most popular and effective techniques for catching crappie.

Brush piles and stumps and their root systems aren't the only hangouts for crappie. There are countless other underwater structures which attract fish. Some of these are old creek and stream beds, rows of fence posts, rock piles, road beds, drainage ditches, some railroad grades, sunken bridges, foundations, old duck blinds—or any channel, gully, or man-made cut that has been flooded.

All these structures, whether they occur naturally or are man-made, provide the basic necessities for crappie—food, protection from larger predators, shade from the sun, and in the case of depressions, cooler temperatures during the hot summer months.

The undulating bottoms of reservoirs are especially well-suited for crappie. When the reservoir begins to form, encroaching waters first swallow up bottomlands near creeks, rivers, and sloughs. Next, the small hills and valleys are flooded leaving only the taller hills protruding above the surface. Thus, water depths may vary considerably in a reservoir, from shore to more than 100-foot depths. Lake Cumberland near Jamestown, Kentucky, has one spot over 350 feet deep.

This brings up an important point for summer crappie anglers to remember. As summer arrives, wind velocities decrease and the sun's rays warm the surface water, causing it to become less dense than the colder water below. As summer progresses, warm surface waters mix to a depth of fifteen to forty feet. Below this warm layer is a zone called the thermocline, varying from five to ten feet where the temperature decreases rapidly. Below the thermocline is a zone called the hypolimnion, where the water is even cooler with little or no oxygen to support game fish.

In big fertile reservoirs, angling the hypolimnion layer is a waste of time, as fish cannot survive there. However, in the big prairie reservoirs where winds continually mix the water, no thermocline may develop and fish may thrive at greater depths.

With these facts in mind, the crappie angler should try to locate structures in water depths from ten to twenty-five feet during summer and fall, but seldom any deeper. An electronic depth finder, contour

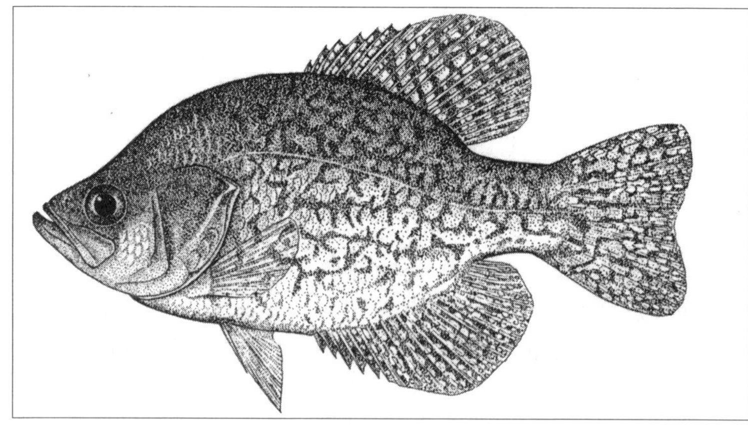

Black crappie.

map of the reservoir and old topographic maps of the watershed before it was impounded are valuable fishing aids.

For example, an excellent place to find crappie is a hump or hill that has been flooded. Water depth over one of these "hogbacks" may be only sixt to fifteen feet while all around this sunken island; the bottom may plunge to thirty or forty feet.

These places are popular feeding spots for big schools of crappie which dine on crawfish, shad and other minnows. Finding one of these spots is like finding that proverbial pot of gold. But there's no rainbow to guide you. Instead, the best way to find a sunken island is with a map and a depth finder.

There are many other reservoir structures which anglers can locate without a depth finder, though a bottom contour map is needed. Rock and gravel shorelines that drop away quickly, riprap banks along dams, roads, and channels, brushy coves, deepwater arms between islands or wherever creeks, small streams, and rivers enter the reservoir— all should produce fish.

Many anglers prefer to hug the shoreline where they fish in and around willows or other trees that have fallen into the water. On the prairie reservoirs anglers bounce a little lead-bodied spinner jig off overhanging rock escarpments to allow the lure to flutter straight down to crappie schools in the depths below.

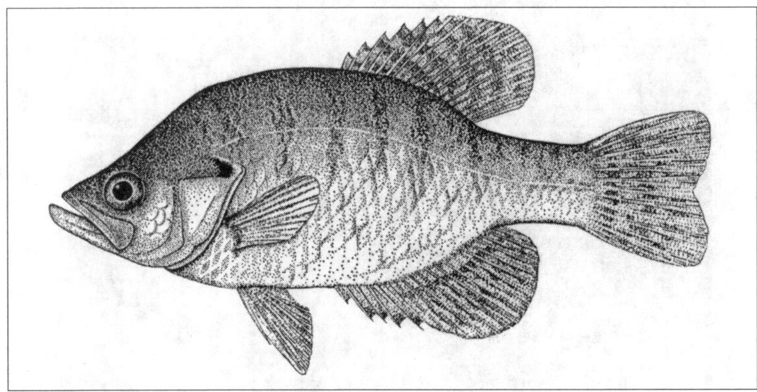

White crappie.

The best crappie fishing reservoirs are vast and complex, often making it difficult for the newcomer to locate fishable schools. And so, the best advice is to inquire with local marina operators, resorts, state park officials or other anglers as to the best spots. The other angler won't be so obliging as to tow you direct to their favorite brush pile. But more times than not, they will point over several good areas. Then, the rest is up to you!

Chapter Fifteen

Rivers and Streams . . .
Horizons Lost

Cold fingers of darkness clutched at our campsite and the entire length of the riverbank as if reaching out in a last, dying grasp. Across the river a morning sun sent beams of light slicing through the treetops.

It was our third and last day on the muddy old river. We were anxious to be on our way. Soon, tent stakes were pulled, a breakfast of wild rice pancakes and bacon was devoured, and our jonboats were launched.

The river's current had lost none of its powerful grip. The murky waters swished and swirled about us, gently tugging our boats into position some thirty feet from shore.

The morning hours raced by. The smallmouth bass, for some unexplained reason, were not caught up by the mystical qualities of this summer morn. Instead they sulked and refused to bite.

But who cared! The air was invigorating. The sound of rushing water playing on the rocks was music to our ears, and life was all around us—frogs, turtles, a regal blue heron, a colorful pair of wood ducks. As we drifted under an old cottonwood, three young great horned owls hooted a "Hello" from the green canopy above.

The magic of this wilderness setting continues to amaze newcomers to this, the granddaddy of all rivers. Al Spiers, then outdoor editor for *Nixon Newspapers* in Michigan City, Indiana, and George Tilford, at that time outdoor editor for the *Indianapolis News*, were admittedly awed that this stretch of the Mississippi River, located within thirty

Most crappie anglers ignore our nation's rivers. Two exceptions are these fishermen, who discovered fast action on the meandering Mississippi River.

miles of a million people in metro Minneapolis and St. Paul, still retained such a lovely wild character.

Later, at lunch, I explained to my enraptured guests that the Upper Mississippi was no different than thousands of other rivers and streams in America. Nearly all provide outstanding scenery and good sport fishing for smallmouth bass, catfish, sunfish, walleye, crappie, and any number of angling favorites from trout to carp and suckers.

But I reminded them that, from cactus country to the cornbelt, our streams are in a state of siege. There is the omnipresent threat of pollution along with a never-ending flow of engineering plans to ditch, dam and channel our rivers. New housing developments also post a serious threat.

With lunch and our discussion ended, we headed downriver on the last segment of our three-day journey. Little did these anglers realize that some of the best fishing was saved for last.

Over the past decade, our "Old Man River Float Trips" have provided unexcelled fishing for anglers from over thirty-five states. Usually smallmouth are literally jumping into the boat. But on those occasional days when the bass prove stubborn, there's always plenty of crappie to be caught in one of my favorite fishing holes, "Rocking Chair Pool."

A few miles south of Monticello, the Mississippi River widens and slowly bends to flow around two beautiful islands. Just above the topmost island, the river gurgles past a rocky, tree-studded point where the water depth drops abruptly from six to twelve feet. This is Rocking Chair Pool, where in sixteen years of fishing I have never failed to catch at least a half-dozen crappies per visit.

This gentle spring day on the "Old Miss" would be no different. We anchored on the perimeter of the pool and tied on small Pinky jigs. Minnows aren't needed here. The first cast by Al Spiers brought a whoop and a holler, "Fish on!" Soon, a nice mess of white crappie were in our live wells.

Rocking Chair Pool is just one of thousands of crappie hotspots in our nation's rivers. Streams such as the Mississippi in Minnesota, Wisconsin, Iowa, and southward; the famous Shenandoah in Virginia; the Missouri and Platte Rivers in Nebraska and Missouri; the Tennessee River in Kentucky and Tennessee; and the Willamette in Oregon consistently produce excellent stringers of crappie.

Interestingly, fishery biologists tell us that many of the best crappie streams do not have permanent breeding populations of slabbies. Instead, the fish are transitory visitors that move from lakes into smaller streams in spring and eventually into larger rivers where they are entrapped. Other crappie populations end up in our rivers during flooding in spring and fall.

On one point I must differ with biologists, however. During spring on the upper reaches of the Mississippi, often only one or two crappies occupy a pool with no other fish apparently in the area. Sometimes there will be an extra male, but in most cases, there are usually just two fish—presumably a male and a female.

Fishery experts claim that crappies "bed" in large communes. But in rivers, I believe, this doesn't always hold true, possibly because good spawning habitat is lacking. What spawning areas exist are all spread out.

Angling success on rivers and streams depends primarily on the angler's ability to recognize good crappie habitat. Pools are gathering areas for crappie because cover, food and often cooler water temperatures are present.

Both pools and small pockets (depressions gouged out by the stream behind rocks and logs) will appear as a darker color than the surrounding water. When working these areas, drop the lure at the tail end of the pool, gradually moving your casts further upstream. This prevents crappie from being spooked from their watery lair.

Probably the best stream habitat for crappie is the tree that has fallen so that part of its complex branching system lies submerged. The branches below the surface provide underwater cover, and those dangling above provide shade.

These areas are often difficult to fish, but for every snag, there is also a silver trophy for the frying pan. My advice for this type of fishing is: be patient and thorough. Here, a lure is seldom needed. Simply dangle any live bait such as a minnow, small crawfish, or cricket. Casting a lure will produce fish, but the thick tangle of branches will generate too many snags.

Flooded Timber Means Crappie A-Plenty

Loads of good eating in a stringer of fish like these.

A stringer limit taken from flooded timber and old river channels.

Newly flooded timber is always good in April, May, and June.

Now here's a pair of dandy black crappie. Really deep water timber fish.

Underwater obstructions such as sunken logs and rocks are gathering places for calico. If float fishing, cast the lure about ten feet ahead of the snag. Then, use both your rod and reel and the current to bring your lure into the pocket of calm water behind the object. Underwater obstructions can be recognized by the "V" they cut on the water surface.

As a river goes about its meandering business, the current slowly erodes the river bank, gouging out the soil to create small, recessed areas. Crappies snuggle back under these overhanging banks, again for the same reasons—food, cover, and shade.

Overhangs are popular with crappies, but they are often extremely difficult to fish. If bank fishing, stand about ten to fifteen feet upstream and then, keeping the rod tip close to the bank or plunging it into the water back toward the bank, slowly let out line until the lure has drifted back under the overhang. The current is usually strong in these areas, so before you attempt this technique, add about a half ounce of weight.

If float fishing, position the boat upstream some twenty to twenty-five feet and allow the lure to settle back under the cutaway bank. The adept angler can cast into these areas, but seldom will the current suck the lure deep within the cavity.

Two other staging areas for crappie deserve mention. Spring holes, or wherever small springs or streams flow into the main river channel, bring cooler water, which has a magnetic effect on crappies. Another good spot is just below dams and waterfalls where strong turbulence creates an abundance of oxygenated water. Barriers, of course, prohibit fish from moving upstream and tend to collect fish.

Yet another hotspot for crappie is the eroded stream bank. Here, crappies gather at different times during the day to feed on worms and other choice morsels that wash down the slippery bank. These areas are also havens for smallmouth bass. Often, the more aggressive bass will strike the lure before crappies will. As a result, the angler often moves on without knowing that the spot also harbors a crappie or two.

Float fishing for crappie and other game fish is, in my opinion, the most enjoyable type of angling. The scenery is varied and constantly changing. Seldom does the lake or reservoir angler see the wildlife that is enjoyed by the "river rat." Even more important, on any given day, no matter what the weather conditions prevail, the river angler will virtually always catch some fish. As you and I can testify, this does not hold true on lakes and large reservoirs where too often the angler goes home skunked.

What is the best crappie stream in the country? Without hesitation, I would choose the Mississippi River. From Minnesota to Missouri, this gentle "old man" offers unparalleled crappie fishing. Unfortunately, the river continues to be ignored by many anglers.

Crappie fishing on the Mississippi can be a year-around affair for the enterprising angler. During spring, look for crappie behind dams or along riprap banks. In summer, fish the deeper sand bars, overhangs, fallen trees, and rocky outcrops extending outward from shore. In fall and winter and on into the early months of spring, crappie are found in the innumerable backwaters of the Mississippi. These large, weed-fringed coves and bays are prime habitat for crappie, even though water may be no deeper than two to ten feet.

The Mississippi and other rivers—such as the Tennessee in Kentucky—provide an extra bonus for crappie anglers each spring. During these flood periods, the rivers overflow their banks to "restock" floodplain lakes with crappie and other species.

Our rivers are untapped treasures for crappie anglers, though the responsibility of all Americans. Our rivers can be popular recreation areas for canoers and anglers, and natural areas for many species of wildlife. Or, they can become dumping grounds for our technological society. The choice is ours . . .

Working a river drop down for fall crappie.

Chapter Sixteen

How to . . . River Crappie

Lord, Dan'l, there ain't been any speks caught on this here river this spring. That's better'n sixty days. Like every year, they just seem to disappear when the water goes down," commented Arthur, the boat dock manager, as he watched me eye the slow-moving river backwater.

"Yeah, Art, I know, but those whitesides have to be here somewhere. They can't just disappear during summer months. The "great-god-of-the-fishes" doesn't just remove them from the river system . . . right?" I retorted.

The bearded old man nodded agreement while moving his cane pole, offering a bobber and garden hackle. Art loved to work the huge sunfish that sought refuge under his dock structure.

"My friend . . . ya could be right. Last night I heard that Jim and Chris Keller, that's those twin boys that live below the big rock point, caught some speks just at dark. Said they took 'em on small floatin' flies just as the sun was a-settin'," Art mumbled while rolling a brown wad of chewing tobacco from right to left.

That made sense! Back home along the upper Mississippi River, north of Minnesota's Twin Cities, the only time crappies could be taken during Augusts' two hottest weeks was at sundown when a good hatch of brown millers was on the rise. The fish would hit both the flies and the minnows drawn to the hatching bugs.

"Art, I think I'm going to give the ol' river a try. A bit of late evening and early night crappie-chasing may be just what it takes!" I happily threw at my friend while heading back to the car for my gear.

There were two hours left before sunset. It was enough time to launch my jonboat and head upstream to an island where deep water channels entered from either side. Here, where willows drooped over eddy surface near island's downstream end, spring crappies were often caught. With river channel depth no deeper than fourteen feet anywhere within eight miles, it was as good a place as any to begin my search.

Art only laughed and made mention that his theory was much easier to believe. Migration downstream must be the answer. I didn't believe it . . . not when fish would have to move better than five miles to reach water only a matter of two feet deeper than that found near their spring spawning grounds.

Over the years I've discovered crappie may migrate far enough to reach comfortable water temperature and acceptable light density but not any further. In most rivers this means only a matter of twenty-five to 150 yards. In rivers, due to rotating waters that keep the surface as

River crappie swin in most of our nation's rivers. Finding them can be a problem if you fail to know where to begin.

well as bottom waters at a constant temperature, crappie may fail to react to water temperatures. They will react to light, however. Thus it is that river crappie can be taken after sunset and hours lasting way into the dark of night.

In many rivers, this theory is never tested due to daylight fishing habits of the angler. Most river fish are known to feed mainly between daylight and dark. Walleye might be the only exception to this rule.

I arrived at the island's lower end just prior to sunset. Quickly the boat bow was tied off to an overhanging willow branch. Behind me, directly downstream, a series of eddies curled this way and that. (See diagram A, this chapter). It was upon these swirling eddy surfaces that an evening hatch of millers would come . . . and it would be to this hatch that crappie would migrate to for food.

And, as if programmed, millers began hatching moments after my arrival. With the millers' appearance, crappie began to gently swirl across eddy surface. An orange ball of sun slowly settled below the horizon.

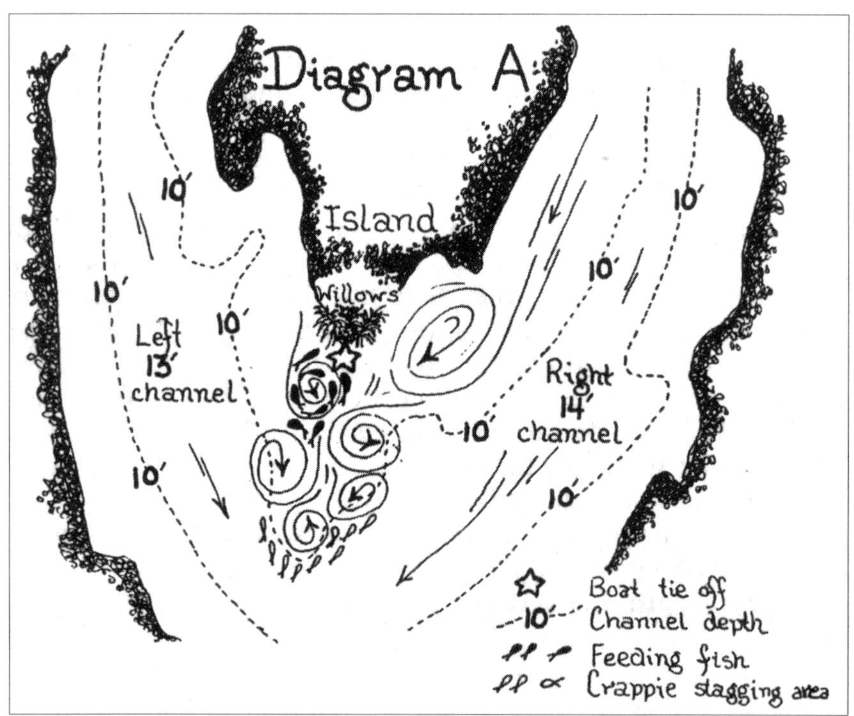

My first cast saw no strike, but cast two with the high-riding dry fly saw it disappear in a soft swish of surface breakage. A near-pound crappie soon slid overboard with a gentle lift of the fly rod. The next five casts brought three more fish. They worked only the flies holding to the very center of the eddy's boil. Any fly that rode the current break along the edge of the eddy was left untouched.

Soon after sunset, as twilight darkened, goodly numbers of crappie could be seen touching the surface. It was time to switch to the spinning outfit. I'd use a small, white marabou jig tied directly to four-pound test monofilament and no tipping minnow.

There was one notable occurrence that transpired as crappie came to feed. Fish action was first observed far out on the eddy's circling surface. As darkness settled, the fish worked in closer to shore. Hatching flies were not the controlling factor on this migration. At first, I could see feeding fish waiting for surface-held flies to be carried far enough out onto eddy structure so they could be eaten. In the end, crappie were finning so close to the rocky shoreline that their dorsal fins exposed themselves above water. At that particular moment, flies hatched far out and close in and just about anywhere an angler might gaze.

The above happenings prevail each time an angler manages to catch Ol' Papermouth in a fly feeding mood. It bears out the migrating travel path that is theorized about such an instance.

Before moving on, let's explore another thought. If crappies station themselves near such an area in any river, why can't you catch them in the daytime? The question has a simple answer. You can!

There is one structure needed to assure daylight success on the holding area noted in Diagram A. At a point where the ten-foot depth chart lines circle point's end, a rather steep incline must occur. It matters little that it doesn't drop more than four feet or so. What matters is that enough incline is attained to create a shaded area off structure. Then, no matter which direction light penetrates, there is a shaded holding area in which crappie might stage.

It is in this shaded area that the daylight angler will find crappie. They will be holding in very tight along the drop, not necessarily as deep as possible, but often a couple feet off the deep side bottom in close on the drop wall.

A search with any electronic depth finder will show you just where this staging structure rests. Look to the willow point structure's most downstream point.

There is another spot in river waterways that put crappie and willow trees together. Often such an area lies along the main stream's flowing portion of the river. Where an angler finds a large willow (weeping style) hugging the riverbank, they will also find crappie throughout most of the season. See Diagram C to follow along.

Willows require a great deal of water to sustain life, thus, a reason for their existence along river waterways. Look for a tree that will hold crappie growing close to waterline, having irregular shoreline upstream and downstream from it, and supporting a small, rotating eddy beneath and downstream from it.

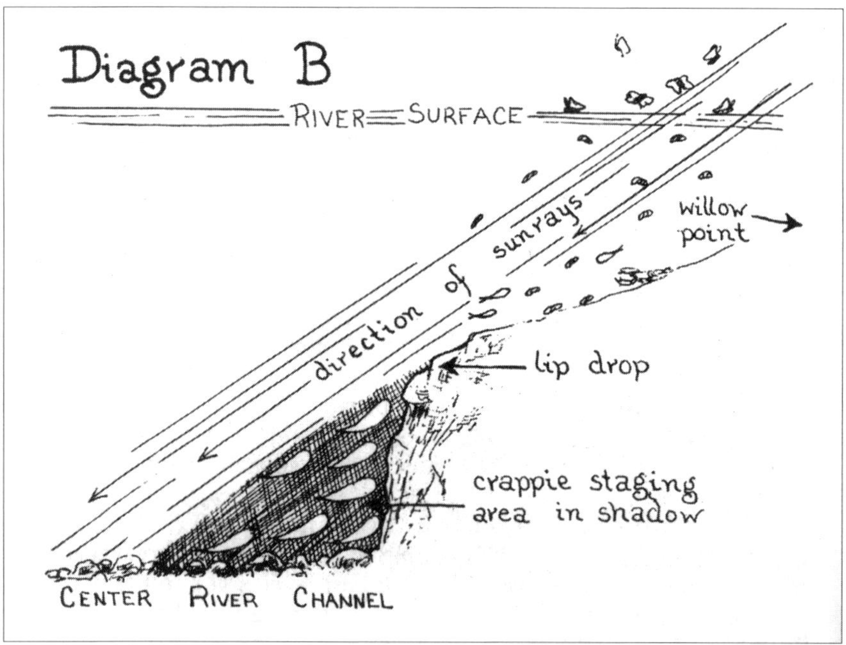

In the spring, spawning crappies are enticed to build nests below the willow's drooping branches. There may be some difficulty when attempting to properly present a lure to these fish. However, a boater will often succeed by tying off to the tree and dabbling a small white jig down through the tree's branches (See Diagram C.) A determined angler who is fairly accurate in their casting might approach the spawning crappie from downstream. The cast and its lure would have to nearly land on shoreline and be worked between hanging willow limbs. For spring river crappie, the use of yellow or chartreuse jigs is a plus, one-thirty-second- and one-sixteenth-ounce are preferred.

This same willow tree will hold crappie throughout most of the summer. By referring once again to Diagram C, you will note summer crappie have now moved out and away from shoreline. They have settled along the current break up under the outer willow branches that lie inundated by water.

These summer fish are best caught during early morning hours or those moments just before sundown and after. In some very cold water streams, crappie might be caught under such structure throughout all daylight hours.

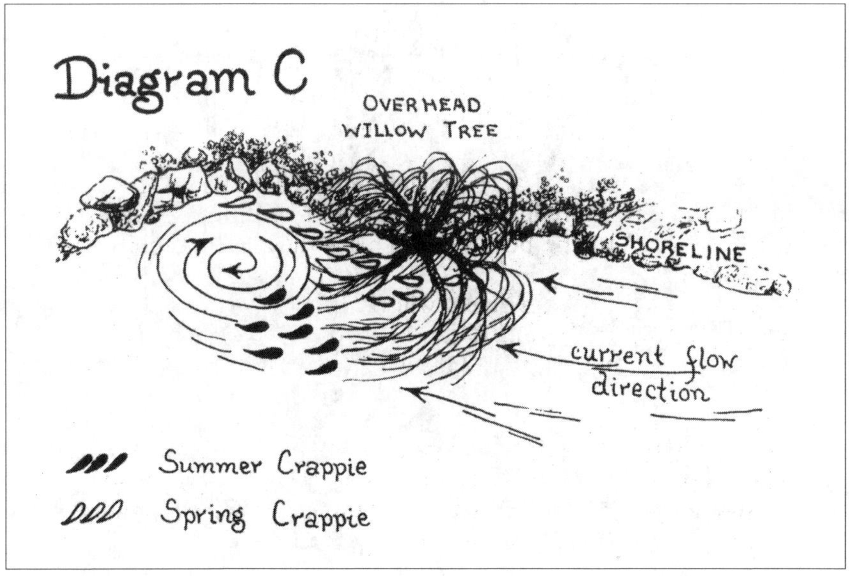

The best fishing approach on these holding fish is to cast up into them from downstream with either bait or "a bit heavier than normal" jig. Retrieve slowly and downstream. If possible, with your boat held steady, an angler might dabble for these willow-tree-held crappie. Once again, live bait (minnow) or jigs will do the job.

Now I want you to refer to Diagram D. It is a typical shoreline scene found along almost any river in the country. In the diagram I have attempted to point out the key spots for crappie throughout the summer season.

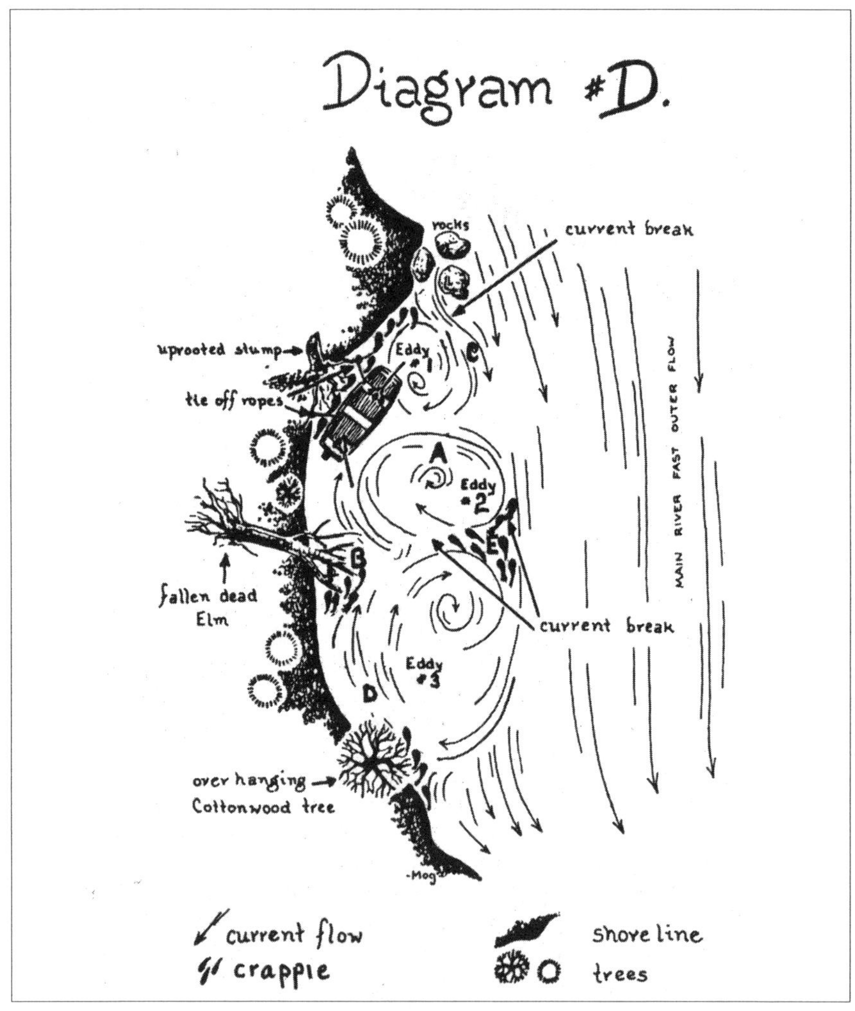

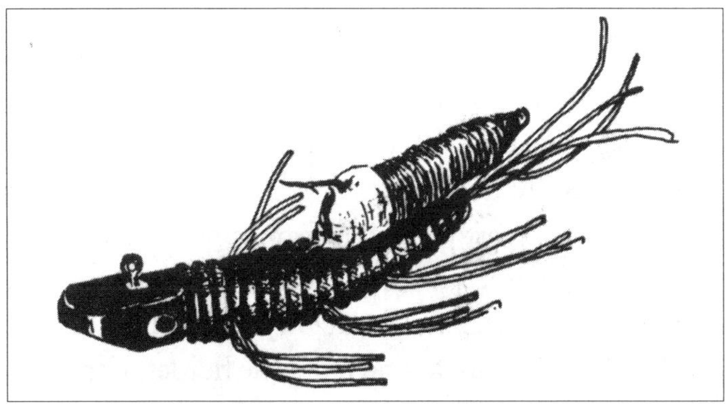

Ugly Bug jig baited with a piece of nightcrawler is a deadly crappie killer too.

But before we begin, I must tell you of a little gadget I use on my river boat that is an immense help. Where the boat is anchored near shoreline along eddy #1, you will see the words, "tie-off rope" to the boat's left. This is the gadget. You will see it in Diagram E.

Any boat that fishes rivers will find such a tie-off rope at either end a very valuable tool. It can be made easily. About thirty minutes of your time and about $2.00 worth of rope and hardware goes into it.

First, an eyebolt is bolted into the boat gunwale. To this eye, a section of rope (twenty-four to thirty-six inches) is attached. To the rope's loose end, a quick clip snap is tied. That's it . . . you're ready to tie off to almost any type of bank structure! By observing Diagram E, this gadget's function is easily noted. With such a rope at either end on your boat (on both sides,) your river fishing will be made much easier!

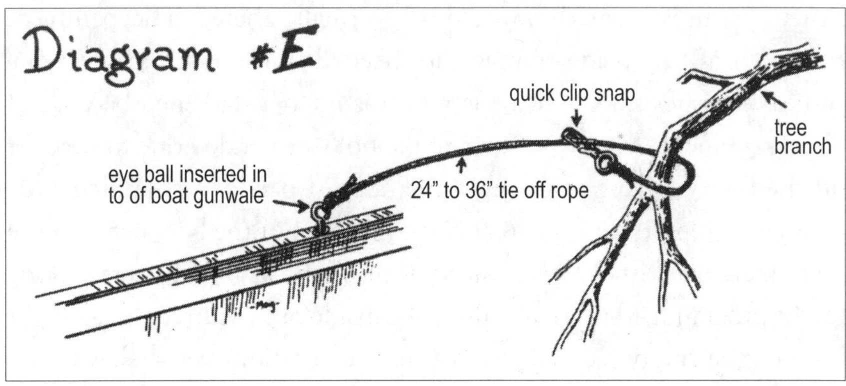

Diagram D has four prominent staging areas for spring and summer crappie. The first is a spring spawning nest area. Spawning crappie will be found along the shoreline side of eddy #1. The fish will fin in water as shallow as eight inches or as deep as three feet. Their spawning range will run from downstream on the stump to the area at the pool's head. It is this type of weed that a great many river crappie spawn in.

A second staging area is that below the fallen dead elm. Soon after spawning, hungry crappie search out the hordes of spring-hatched minnows that migrate to this structure. Minnows come for bugs and larvae which dead trees produce. Crappie will hold around this structure until water warms and summer light penetration drives them off. The best time to work area B is early morning and late evening. It is an ideal place that can provide excellent fly fishing for crappie.

Below the area marked D on Diagram D, there is an overhanging cottonwood tree. Though it rests far down from where an angler might suspect crappie to lie, this structure can and does produce excellent summer late-day angling. Once again, food in the form of minnows come for the bug hatches produced by the cottonwood tree. This area may produce best after sunset or even after dark. As is the custom in most crappie staging areas, small white, yellow or silver jigs produce well. This area may see small crankbaits do a number on crappie.

Between eddy #2 and #3 where I've marked an area E along the main current cut, you will find the best overall crappie staging area this diagram has to offer. If there are any numbers of crappie holding in the structure, this is where they would be. Normally, there is a deepening of river bottom to provide crappie with needed shade. And, with circling eddies on either side, light penetration is further darkened because of their movement. In most cases, crappie hold suspended one to two feet off the bottom. This normally is the deepest part of a shoreline eddy structure. To produce fish, an angler could anchor the boat between the point marked eddy #3 and the words "current break." From here, casting can be programmed upstream along the inside of the current break, right through the crappie school. Work your presentation ever so slowly.

One more thing about the E staging area. These fish are often seen to migrate in toward point B as sunset occurs. If this doesn't occur, you may find their numbers split and migrate to the near center of eddy #2 and eddy #3. At these points, they feed on hatching flies. Another excellent opportunity for fly fishing.

For those of you who fish the smaller rivers where crappies reside, Diagram F shows spring spawning grounds as well as the typical summer holding areas. In small streams, crappies are sometimes difficult to locate. Many anglers feel they are best caught after dark during all seasons of the year. That may be partly true, but if the angler is persistent, crappie can be taken during daylight hours. On many small rivers and streams such as this diagram indicates, small, short, shore-hugging weeds are seen to grow in pools that indent the shoreline below many of the fast waters. They grow close to shore and seldom exist in water deeper than twenty-four inches. Here, among weedy habitat, an angler finds spring-spawning crappie.

When crappie spawn, they lose much of their normal caution when feeding. The males strike everything and anything that gets in their way. Anglers using a small bobber with a one-thirty-second-ounce white jig suspended under it some six to ten inches will clean up on these spawning fish. There is little need to give this combination any motion or action. The crappie will come immediately to it once it is spotted. Flourescent yellow jigs also work well.

Refer to Diagram F. In many cases, these small shallow-water weeds extend from point #1 to point #3 on a long eddy such as shown on the left. They may also be noted in narrow deep bays such as diagrammed at point #2 in the right hand bay. Crappie will be well scattered throughout the weeds at depths varying from six inches to two feet.

Once spawning passes, the crappie will migrate out into the stream system. Look for them to stage at point #4 and #5 on Diagram F. The hotter summer temperatures become, the more likely crappies will refrain from feeding near dark or after dark. Water depth can vary extensively for the fish holding on points #4 and #5. In small streams, it may be only a matter of a drop from two feet to four feet.

There are other places that provide excellent crappie staging areas in a river system. These have only been a few but considered some of the best!

Chapter Seventeen

Where Crappie Is King

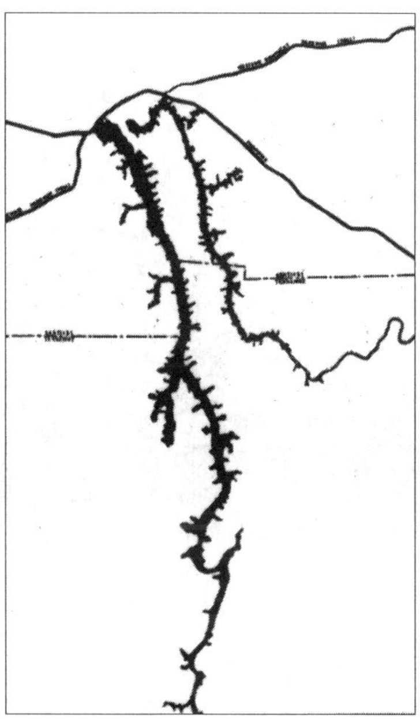

The nation's best . . . Kentucky (left) and Barkley lakes. Innumerable "fingers" and coves provide outstanding fishing.

Every avid crappie angler has his or her favorite fishin' hole. They range from Possum Kingdom Lake in Texas to Swinging Bridge Reservoir in New York State. It may be Coffee Pot Lake in Washington, or Raccoon Reservoir in Indiana, or maybe Surprise Lake in New Jersey.

Today, nearly every state in the continental U.S.A. offers some crappie fishing, though not all have outstanding crappie waters.

Is there one lake that ranks above all others for its crappie fishing? In selecting the nation's outstanding crappie lake, several factors were weighed. The lake must be large enough and with sufficient recreational facilities to accommodate many fishermen. It must have a large crappie population with liberal limits. It must be accessible and easy to fish, even for the novice angler. Because of the gas prices, it must be in relatively close proximity of a large number of people.

Certainly there are countless lakes which meet some of these criteria. But only one, in our opinion, meets and exceeds all of the requirements in addition to providing numerous other recreational amenities for anglers. That lake is huge Kentucky Lake located partly in the states of Kentucky and Tennessee.

Kentucky Lake rises behind a Tennessee Valley Authority dam completed in 1944 to regulate floods on the lower Ohio and Mississippi rivers. Located on the Tennessee River, the dam creates a reservoir 184 miles long with a volume of six million acres of water.

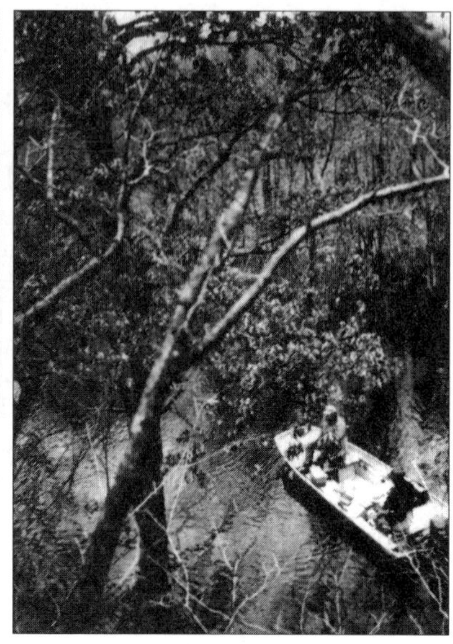

Anglers on Lake Livingston in Texas (above) and Kentucky Lake (right) know where the action is . . . the flooded timberlands and narrow, water-filled ravines.

A visit to beautiful Kentucky Lake in spring is an unforgettable experience. Crappie anglers are everywhere. Fishing rods bristle from the windows and luggage racks of cars and campers like quills on a porcupine. Everywhere there are boats—from simple jonboats to the fancy "pro" bass boats outfitted with more electronic equipment than a nuclear sub.

In the morning, many of the lake's twenty accesses are jammed with cars, trailers, and boats. But amazingly, within hours it seems the vast lake has swallowed them up. Some anglers with smaller boats and motors remain near the accesses, fishing shallow bays in coves. But many others venture as far as five miles back into any of the lake's numerous "arms," those long woodland ravines that have been inundated.

Fishing is fast and furious. Anglers who discover flooded broomsedge weeds, blackberry briars, and cockleburs in the shallows are often the first to reach their limit. Others who dabble jigs and minnows around sunken treetops, brush piles, boat harbors, and docks have little difficulty in catching large stringers of "silver perch," the moniker given to white crappie in this neck of the woods.

Reservoirs provide year-round fishing fun for thousands of fishermen.

Toward evening boat after boat returns with limit or near-limit catches of crappie. As the heavy stringers are brought ashore, one begins to wonder if the lake's crappie population is in danger of extinction. By returning the next day and the next, that question is shrugged off as bordering the ridiculous, for one soon learns that Kentucky Lake's crappie population is inexhaustible.

Kentucky Lake, no matter the season, is unsurpassed for crappie either in quantity or quality. Its waters have produced many near-record-breaking sizes over the years.

But Kentucky Lake and nearby Barkley Lake offer more than just top-quality fishing. The picturesque woods sandwiched between the two lakes has been set aside as a recreation area for camping, hunting, exploring and bird watching. This 170-acre peninsula, known as Land Between the Lakes, contains numerous trails and even a conservation education center to help visitors discover the fragile beauty of the woods and the creatures that inhabit it.

The Tennessee portion of Kentucky Lake is just as varied and exciting. Here, several state parks, a wildlife management area and the Tennessee National Wildlife Refuge offer uncountable outdoor experiences for those of intrepid spirit.

But of singular importance is the location of Kentucky Lake, within a day's drive of some eighty million Americans, a factor which is especially important at this time of high gasoline prices.

Crappie fishing at Kentucky Lake need not be a wallet-shrinking experience. Many areas are accessible for shore fishing. Finding crappie from a boat is simply a matter of finding other crappie anglers. There are guides available, and, after a day or two with one of these experts, the angler may strike out on their own. Licenses too are not expensive.

Yet another important factor considering Kentucky Lake is that it offers a more-than-adequate number of marinas, boat

Huge crappie taken from fallen log structure along old river bed. Note . . . the live crappie in the boat's livewell.

ramps, campgrounds, picnic areas, and nearby cabins and motels to accommodate untold numbers of anglers. Information on these facilities along with a wealth of crappie fishing facts can be obtained by contacting: TVA at tvainfo@tva.com or calling (865) 632-2101 or Kentucky Department of Parks at www.parks.ky.gov or calling (800) 255-7275.

Now that we've named our top crappie lake, it's certainly apropos to select the outstanding crappie state.

In 1957 the state of Mississippi became the focal point of the crappie fishing fraternity when a world-record white crappie was taken from Enid Reservoir in Panola County.

The Magnolia State does not hold a monopoly on crappie fishing, but there the spunky little panfish reigns as king of fishes. Mississippi has five sprawling reservoirs—three of which boast more than 30,000 acres each. In addition, the state claims at least another dozen excellent crappie waters.

Nice black crappie caught alongside the flooded tree top shown.

Probably the most spectacular angling is found in 30,000-acre Ross Barnett Reservoir, which laps over five Mississippi counties. During high water of January, thousands of pounds of crappie are pulled from the backwater near the lake's spillway. Another potential hotspot is the state's newest major impoundment, Okatibbee Reservoir near Meridan. Here, crappie fishing continues to improve year-to-year.

The state of Mississippi deserves credit not only for its abundance of crappie, but for its dedication to managing lakes to maintain quality fishing. The Game and Fish Commission places "fish mats" on selected lakes to concentrate crappie and other sport fish, thus enhancing the fishing success for anglers. Also, it has constructed fishing piers for children and the physically handicapped.

In our research for this book, we discovered many other states with outstanding fish management programs, especially with regard to crappie and crappie fishing.

In my previous book on crappies, there was a long list of the nation's leading crappie waters, state by state. I will not attempt such a task again. Through my years, the one thing that has been learned is the fact that crappie waters change from year to year. There are but two reservoirs that consistently produce record crappie year in and

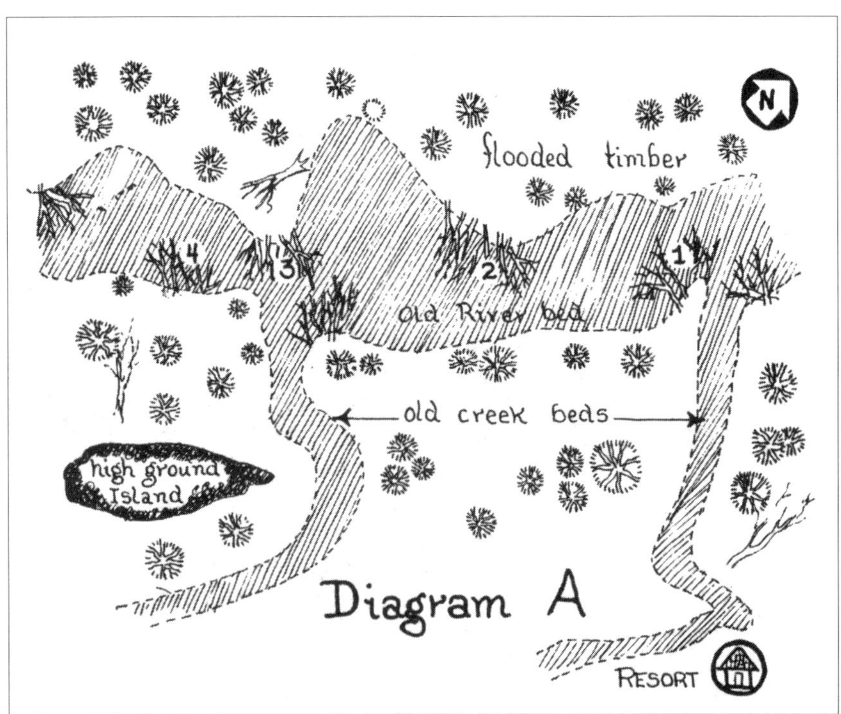

year out. One we have elevated to fame at the beginning of this chapter . . . the other I will now detail.

What is the second heaviest crappie producer?

Choice two is none other than Toledo Bend Reservoir on the Texas/Louisiana border. This 182,000-acre reservoir has to be the best for producing that once-in-a-lifetime monster! Oh, there are those new impoundments that get "hot" but these also soon cool off. You might get lucky in such water, but if you want to bet money on one piece of water in North America, it would be Toledo Bend.

Several years ago my brother, Joe, a fellow who could care less about Ol' Papermouth, and I had the opportunity to work the entire length of Toledo Bend Reservoir. Of course, Joe's target fish was the huge bass reported to exist in these waters. As always, I'd take anything that came my way.

Day one saw our search begin near the reservoir's southern end and gradually work north. Most of our fishing was concentrated along the western shoreline. Here, a network of bays and inlet estuaries pro-vided what locals called "good ol' hog territory!" Unfortunately no one had told the hogs. Joe and I failed to catch a bass over four pounds in two days of exploring.

The morning of day three saw our sturdy jon-boat hit the water at a private resort launching site. The resort's name now escapes me. However, its overall design was of similar style to that used on most of the resorts along the

Pound and a half to near three-pound crappie taken off flooded timber.

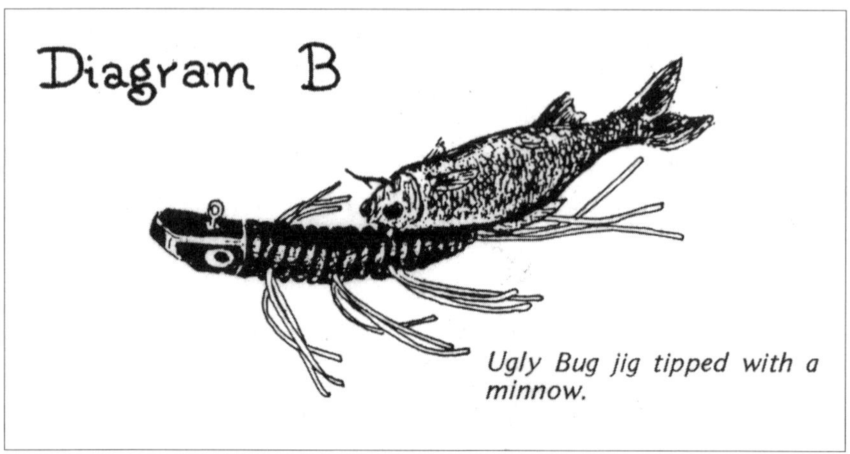

Ugly Bug jig tipped with a minnow.

flood plain reservoir boundaries. Main building was of metal construction built high on stilts while individual cabins were basically small travel trailers on wheels. From the way they were built, it was obvious they could be moved as flooding occurred. Yard décor consisted of weeds, broom straw, and powdery sand/clay roadways.

A query of the resort owner brought my "Hog Happy" brother face to face with the reality that it might be possible we'd not take a bass worth keeping this day or during any of our three remaining days.

"Yeah . . . bassin' has been tough lately, fellas. Got to get here earlier or closer to spring if you want big 'uns," responded the bayou woman named Fern.

Where haven't I heard those words before?

"But if'n you want to get into 'speks', they're running fairly big along the ol' creek bed at center channel," Fern advised as Joe now gazed down into the resort's bait tank. A last thought tempted his Puritan soul.

"You mean crappies, don't you?" I responded.

"Yup . . . down here they grown bigger'n 'craaapie' . . . we call 'em speks," our host joshed while selecting a fresher chaw of chewing tobacco to replace the one she'd just deposited in a dark corner.

"What've they been hittin'?" I asked, a ray of hope now lifting my anticipation.

"Minnows seem to be best . . . but they tell me just about anything will do," Fern answered.

That was it!

"Joe . . . you do what you want, but your brother is buying some minnows. I'm tired of catching those 'one jumpers.' Furthermore, we haven't caught a third as many as we might have had we been back on a Minnesota lake," I instructed.

Three dozen plus minnows were dropped into a broken Styrofoam minnow bucket, and within minutes we were off. Where the old creek bed hit the old river bed, we had no idea, but if it was like most of these flooded timber-lined reservoirs, it should be easily picked out. The old river bed would be that structure of water that wandered aimlessly through the reservoir's center where no dead trees held above surface. The creek bed that began directly in front of the resort would be similarly identified.

Sure enough! By following tree skeletons along the creek bed, Joe and I found a meandering ribbon of open water that headed roughly

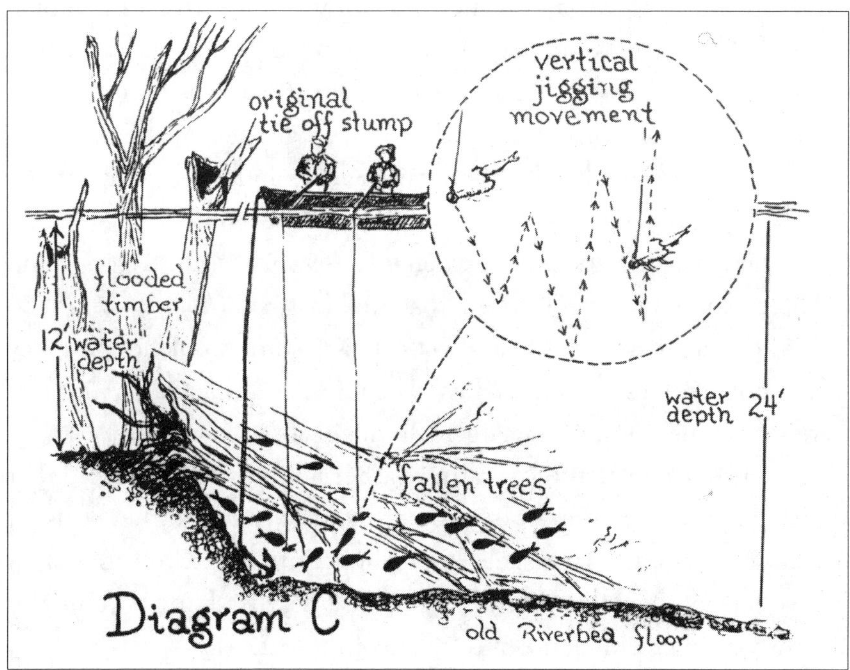

north and south. This would be the original river bed. Water depth plunged from twelve to fifteen feet into nearly thirty-two feet at the old river center.

If you've not fished topside of Toledo Bend, there is an adventure in fishing yet to come your way. Unlike most reservoirs, upper Toledo Bend had few, if any, of its resident trees removed prior to flooding. Thus, wherever you look bleached tree skeletons protruded above water in varying degrees of height. Near the reservoir's northern end, there are countless square miles of flooded tree bones. As you gradually travel south where the reservoir depth deepens, these same tree skeletons can only be found in the backwaters and coves. Along the southern end, there are very few water-killed trees. Those once there long ago submerged and rotted away below Toledo's deepening waters.

Many, if not most, of the manmade reservoirs in North America had much, if not all, of their existing timber lumbered prior to flooding. For some reason Toledo Bend Reservoir was allowed to hold her natural foliage. In so doing, excellent fish habitat was created . . . habitat that is now more than excellent . . . for when you think of crappie grounds, there can be none better than flooded foliage in the form of trees. Such habitat produces insects that in turn cause minnows to flourish, which in turn draws and produces crappies by the millions.

Upon reaching the old main river bed, Joe and I elected to fish the submerged main channel points where the heaviest timber once stood.

Our reasoning was simple; when the reservoir was first flooded and as these exposed river points were battered by surface winds, an undercutting of main bank would have occur. This, in turn, would topple many of the point's trees into the old river bed. (Refer to Diagram A.) It was here that we felt most of the larger fish might station themselves.

By using an electronic locating flasher it was soon discovered that our theory was accurate. At each outer bend of river bed there existed a lean-to of sloping tree skeletons. Their butts appeared to rest in twelve feet of water while the tops were towards channel center in depths varying from eighteen to twenty-four feet.

Fern had mentioned that fish were being taken at the point where her leading creek bed met the old river bed (See point #1 on Diagram A.) After a couple sweeps over the entry point, it was easily understood. On either side, where small points once existed, there now rested a pair of log piles some twelve feet below water surface.

Joe and I tied off onto a dead tree stump as close to point #1's main river bed's end as possible. From here we would be able to cast toward deep water and retrieve into shallow along the fallen tree structure.

With three dozen fresh minnows waiting to serve our bobbers, you may not understand our next move. Joe and I chose to place artificial jigs at our lines' end. I'd use the traditional one-sixteenth-ounce white hair jig while Joe selected a one-eighth-ounce chartreuse rubber-legged jig I invented called the Ugly Bug.

If you've not fished deep water timber before, I can attest to one fact; you're bound to get snagged . . . snagged a goodly number of times! And, you're going to lose some lures. So it was with Joe and I before we discovered that vertical jigging would do just as good a job of fooling fish. Joe's Ugly Bug jig was snagged far less than my round-headed jig model, but even the Bug's specially-designed head wouldn't keep it off all the snaggy hang ups. Cast three for brother Joe brought the familiar line tightening that meant crappie strike. It's sort of a "sucking up of lure" pull that all crappie anglers get to recognize. Joe quickly hefted up and against his light open-face to see the fish clear itself of the submerged timber. Once in open water, the sturdy fish brought a better than average fight (for a crappie.) On the scale our first crappie weighed in at two pounds, one ounce. It was Joe's biggest crappie ever!

"My gawd, Joe, that's some kind of fish. Do you realize it's our first crappie, and it's bigger by seven ounces than any crappie you've ever taken up home (a reference to our black crappie in Minnesota)?" I questioned as my brother admired his first fish.

"And, you know, that fish is nearly as big as any bass we've taken in the last three days," I further stated. It was true! Joe's first crappie was deep, long, and big-mouthed. Its measurements, with the exception of width were equivalent to our largest bass, a near four-pounder.

Fifteen minutes later, both Joe and I had had enough of snagging up. We changed our method of angling. Both styles of jigs would be rigged "Minnesota" style. To accomplish this, a minnow had to be "tipped" abroad the jig's single hook (see Diagram B.)

Note: When "tipping" jigs with minnows, always insert the hook point directly between the eyes and slightly back up the forehead. Your hook point should then exit along the lower jaw near center between gill cover closings. Such a tipping procedure will see a minnow firmly embedded on your jig hook, allowing numerous casts and retrieves. Were the angler to insert his jig hook through the lower part of the minnow's head (the soft spot,) it would easily rip and disengage. However, a minnow's upper head is hard and boney, and when pressure is placed with cast or retrieve, it is done so here at this point. Thus it is that a minnow's head bone becomes important in this style of fishing.

Brother Joe loosened the rope leading to the stump and allowed us to drift out over the submerged tree bodies. Here an anchor was dropped. We would vertically jig our offerings directly under the boat. What we were about to do wasn't that unusual. Vertical jigging, no matter what it's called—spatting, bowlowing, flipping or jerking—is an excellent way to take structure-hidden crappie or suspended fish.

By referring to Diagram C, the reader will easily see how such a technique works. Once our anchor was solidly embedded in the river bed, we dropped lure offerings overboard. Once our minnow-tipped jigs touched the bottom, they were immediately raised into suspension and worked ever so slowly as Diagram C indicates. Jigging motion, as is the case in most crappie fishing modes, was done softly while passing through a limited amount of space. There is little need to entice crappie in a manner similar to that used on other game fish. This fish likes slow-moving targets that taste like minnows.

From the spot marked #1, we took better than a dozen fish that ranged in weight from one and a quarter to two and a half pounds. All were released.

At our next stationing point, #2, we took mostly fish over two pounds. The tree sub-structure seemed longer and deeper. That could have been the reason for the larger crappie size. Fish on this structure were also fooled on the Ugly Bug jig minnow combo. Here we used one-eighth- and one-quarter-ounce sizes, with colors that ranged from yellow through blue and chartreuse.

In the general area, we caught lots more fish. Some we kept, some released. You can only eat so many, you know. And, during our remaining days on Toledo Bend Reservoir, we continued to fish the upper north end where late fall weather held and crappie with mouths like bass continued to come to the net. The white crappie in Toledo Bend have huge mouths. Some of the fish caught had a mouth opening that I could actually place my hand in. Our biggest tipped the scale at three pounds, ten ounces.

That's some kind of horse.

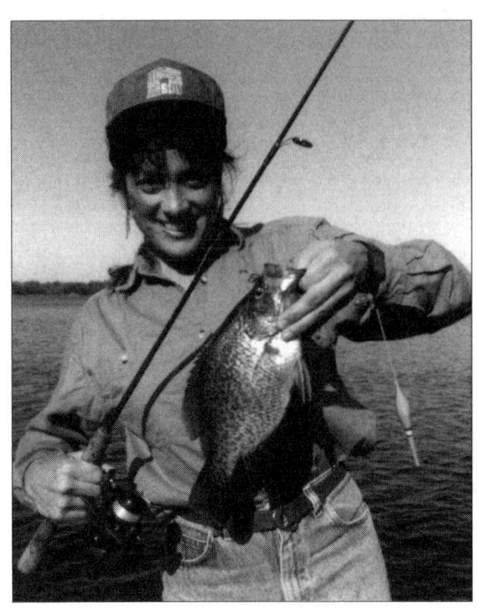

Chapter Eighteen

It's All about Panfish and Farm Ponds

I watched "Bobber" Anne as her eyes riveted on her float just in front of the shore-line lilies. Water reached a depth near four feet where she placed her Slip-n-Lock float loaded with a small crappie-sized fathead minnow. Suddenly she squinted, and a soft smile crossed her face.

The bobber was down!

Gently she raised her rod to engage the fish that had swallowed her offering. The smell of rosebuds was in the air. It was panfish time in the shallows on Monroe Reservoir.

It had been nearly forty years since I last visited Monroe. At that time Bayou Bill Scifres, George Emmelman, and the reservoir manager, Tom, whose last name escapes me now had come to the newly formed Indiana body of water near Bloomington to open the bass season. Along with largemouth bass, the state had planted the new reservoir with white and black crappie, three species of sunfish, and shad as a forage fish.

We had done well on bass, which ran about two pounds on average. Panfish, especially the red-eared bluegill, were hand-sized and provided as much action as the bass. During a rainstorm on the second day, the four of us crowded to a public bath house situated on a point on the northwest corner of the reservoir, seeking shelter. Here, in a bathoom, the word PLUS was added to the lure Ol' Bill loved so much. We'd been fishing Hairy Worms for bass but found that, when a jig spinner was added, they became doubly effective in the muddy cove waters. I asked the question, "Guys, what am I going to call this new version of the Hairy Worm?"

I went on, "It's a Hairy Worm plus . . . what?" It was then my buddy Bayou Bill came up with an answer. "Dan, you just said it. Call it a Hairy Worm Plus. That will do!"

So it was, the word PLUS became part of the U.S.'s descriptive pronunciation. Two years later the ad agency for Alka-Seltzer came out with Alka-Seltzer Plus. Many of the people in the agency were anglers. The Hairy Worm Plus was one of the agency's employees favorite lure.

Now you know the rest of the story! I've often thought how rich I'd be today if I'd only received one dollar for every time the word PLUS has been used. But being young, the thought of trademarking a word like Plus never crossed my mind.

"Dan, your float's down!" Anne's voice came to disrupt my dreams of days gone by.

Sure enough, upon lifting my rod tip, my float reappeared then disappeared below once again. Anne had succeeded in landing a decent-sized crappie, one large enough to keep and eat. I managed a scrappy red-eared sunfish and both came off the lily pads a couple feet apart.

At one time when I first fished Monroe Reservoir, there were no lily pads to be found. But recent aging of its water and siltation in some of its bays has produced such structure. Like everywhere else, lilies come to older reservoir structures.

We had arrived at that point in time when pre-spawn on both these species was in stage. Even so, immature schools of crappie now held off their spawning grounds. In the case at Monroe, they'd migrate through the newly formed lily pads into the sandy bottom at one foot of depth.

Knowing that pre-spawn crappie will strike at anything, such as artificials, as easily as they will live bait, the two of us switched to tan and gray one-thirty-second-ounce Freshwater Shrimp jigs.

Once in a reproductive mode, crappie tend to visually accept their food and rely less on smell. It's been my opinion for years that their spawning mode leaves them with a lessened sense of smell. Thus their eagerness to take artificial lures.

Dan's granddaughter Cassie with a crappie taken on a pink Freshwater Shrimp.

One thing I must mention here. After years of researching this prolific species, most anglers tend to use white or chartreuse artificial jigs to entice crappie. I've found day in and day out that tan, gray, and pink produce better the year around.

From the time we switched to the natural-colored Freshwater Shrimp under a five-inch Slip-n-Lock crappie float, it was one fish after another. Equal amounts of crappie and red-ears were taken.

FARM POND BLUEGILL, A TEACHING SCHOOL!

Throughout the United States, hundreds of thousands of farm ponds are sprinkled across our land. No matter whether constructed by man or created naturally by nature, these jewels provide some of our nation's best panfishing.

Farm ponds normally consist of a water surface of half of an acre to about four acres. Water depth seldom exceeds more than fifteen feet. Only when a pond has been built by man by damming up a small creek will the depth of a pond go into the twenty-five- to thirty-foot range.

Many natural ponds or farm ponds have been stocked naturally by reproduction via the small streams which feed them. Native species of bass, rock bass, some species of bluegill, and a host of chubs, shiners, fatheads, and bullheads make up the balance. However, man in many cases has stocked the natural ponds with other species.

Man made farm ponds for the most part were constructed as livestock watering reservoirs. Those constructing these water holes tend to want a secondary use for the ponds. Thus, fish were stocked. Largemouth bass, several species of bluegill, catfish, and crappie were chosen. In some cases, in higher altitudes, rainbow, and brown trout were introduced.

The main object was to see the large-mouth population flourish. This was accomplished by the introduction of bluegill, the bass's favorite food. For years, the humans who constructed the ponds benefitted from the resource they'd constructed. Cattle were watered and there were always fish for Friday night dinner!

Man had also created a school for the youth of our nation to be educated in the world of fishing.

I can't say when or where the first child leaned his or her cane pole out over

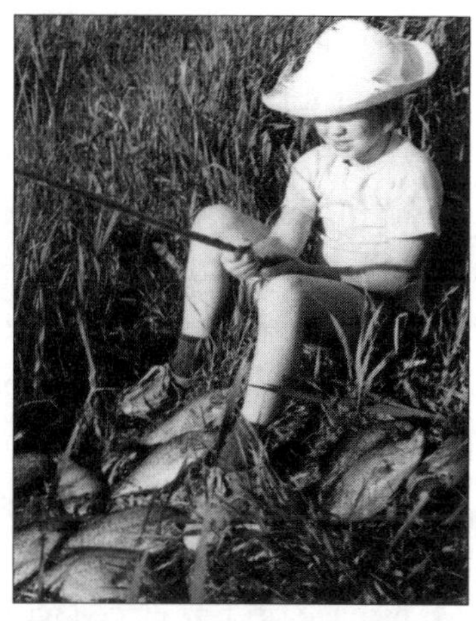

There isn't a better place to start the young angler to fish than a local farm pond.

the still waters of a farm pond, but it surely began in farm country. From Alabama to Oklahoma to Missouri and on up to Indiana, pond fishing flourished. In the beginning children and a cane pole loaded with garden worms did the trick. Then they graduates to the adult bass and became a catfish angler.

Many of the natural ponds, once flooded, swamped large numbers of trees. These in turn became structure on which you could find bass and bluegill staging. The deep end where artificial dams had been constructed held deep water and catfish.

Catching fish in the ponds wasn't hard as long as you followed certain rules. In the spring, in time of spawn, the shallows held panfish and bass alike. It was here that the first weed growth occurred. Lily pads, bulrushes, and flooded hay eventually became spawning structure. The fish population in the ponds flourished.

During summer the dead wood timber became holding structure for bass and crappie. Normal bass and crappie fishing techniques and tackle could be applied with excellent results.

Fall and winter saw the pond fish population crowded into the deepest water. In dammed up creek ponds, species migrate to the bottom end where dam face becomes a structure from which to angle.

On natural ponds and cattle watering dugouts, fish migrate to the deep center region.

Most fishing is done from shore, but in cases where acreage of a pond increased, small jonboats must be used to reach the fish.

Though thousands of modern-day anglers continue its use, these structures, the farm pond is still a place for youngsters to learn. Gone for the most part are the cane poles, replaced by the modern light spinning gear. Garden worms continue to entice the pond species even though the young of today have been schooled in how to use jigs, crankbaits, and spinners. Gone are the bib overalls, the checkered red-and-white shirt. Many have been replaced with tailored shirts with brag patches obtained when the child watched his favorite bass hero on TV.

It matters little what the child fishes with. What matters is the thrill they gain as that first bobber disappears beneath the surface of their favorite farm pond. What matters is the education gained by all those hours spent on his or her favorite pond. What matters is that the fishing world has gained a new member!

The young man (left) will be hooked on fishing after he shows off this stringer to mom and dad, Not to be outdone, this young lady (right) will end life fishing seventy-five years from now . . . It was this stringer of crappie that began her fishing career.

Chapter Nineteen

Crappie Cookout

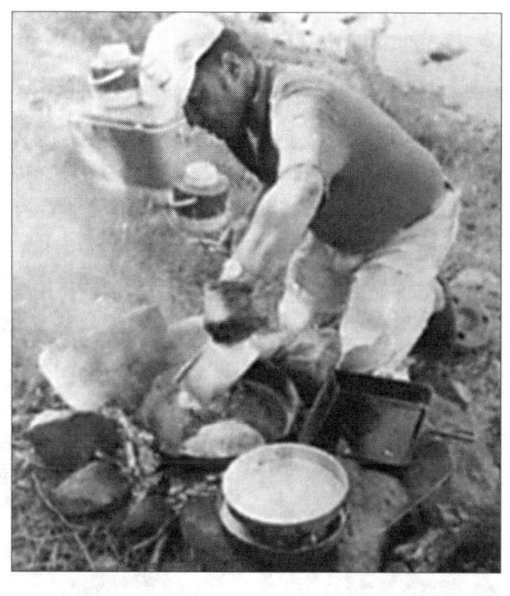

For two days our fishing party of six had been camped at Kentucky Dam State Park on Kentucky Lake where we had caught largemouth bass, crappie, and catfish. On our third and last morning, four of our group headed out to pursue yet another exciting game fish of that region—silver bass. Left behind were tackle representative Bill Hughes, and Gim Dossett of the Kentucky Department of Parks.

While our foursome was away the "dynamic duo" left camp to catch nearly forty crappie, none of which dressed out at less than one pound. Then they prepared the crappie with potato salad and hush puppies (made of cornbread with chopped onions and several other tasty ingredients).

That evening four tired fishermen returned to find dinner—no, call it a feast—already on the table. *What a treat that was!*

Old Gim recalled it best: "Together, that bunch reminded me of an old-fashioned wheat thrasher—you know, wheat going one way, straw the other. Except in this case the chaff was crappie bones. I've never seen six guys eat so much!"

Though I've eaten nearly every species of North American game fish—prepared Heinz 57 ways—I would still have to rank crappie as one of the most delectable freshwater fish.

Crappie can be cleaned easily by several methods and cooked according to any number of mouth-smacking recipes. Size of the fish usually

A keen-edged fillet knife is essential when cleaning a mess of crappie.

determines how you clean it. Larger crappie should be filleted while small fish (six ounces or less) can simply be scaled, gutted and beheaded.

To fillet crappie, grip the fish's mouth and cut down to the backbone just behind the gills. Turn the knife and follow along the backbone toward the tail.

Next, you may either work the knife around the rib cage, or cut through the ribs and remove them later.

Complete the fillet but leave it attached to the tail. Flip the fillet back over the tail and slide the knife between the skin and the meat to skin the fish. The skinning process may seem difficult at first, but will come easier after several fillets. Starting at the tail, work a flexible knife forward in a sawing motion being sure to keep it almost parallel with the fillet board.

Flip the fish over and repeat the procedure.

A big mess of crappie can be cleaned in half the time by using an electric knife. The battery type and cordless works best because there is no cord to get in the way.

For the best in eating, prepare crappie the same day they are caught. However, more often than not you'll want to freeze some or all of your catch.

Probably the best technique for freezing crappie is to dump them into a clean milk container or coffee can, fill it with water and freeze. Be sure that none of the fillets protrude above the water or they will become freezer burned. This method works best when storing fish for long periods and is considered the best technique for retaining the delicate taste and moisture in fresh fish.

Crappie may also be wrapped in heavy-duty freezer paper. Wrap the fish tightly, being careful that all pockets of air are eliminated. Seal the wrap with tape to prevent loosening.

No matter how you freeze your fish, be sure to use a marker to write the type of fish, the date caught, and the approximate amount contained within.

When cooking crappie, the addition of lemon, onions, and spices enhances the eating quality of the fish.

Now, here is what food lovers and that includes all of us, I'm sure, have been waiting for. Following are favorite crappie recipes from near and far . . .

Barbequed Panfish

6 panfish	1½ tablespoon salt
1 egg	1 tablespoon poultry seasoning
1 cup cooking oil	1 teaspoon pepper
½ cup vinegar	1 pinch garlic powder

Beat egg, add cooking oil and beat again. Add remaining ingredients and beat together. Marinate fish for 30 minutes. Wrap marinated fish in aluminum foil and cook over charcoal for 30 minutes.

Beer Batter Crappie

Salt and pepper crappie pieces. Mix together 1 egg, 1 cup warm beer, and 1 cup flour. Dip fillets in batter being sure to cover well. Drop fillets into hot oil deep enough to completely immerse pieces. Fry about 7 minutes.

Baked Crappie

Salt and pepper fillets or pieces on all sides and in the cavity. Place fish side by side in baking dish. Place pats of margarine, sliced onions, tomatoes, and 1 lemon slice on each fish. Bake 30 minutes at 325 degrees with foil covering. The last 10 minutes cover the fish.

Tangy Fried Crappie

Thoroughly clean and scale or fillet crappies. Heat ½ cup margarine in heavy skillet. Add 2 tablespoons prepared mustard, place fillets in pan and sauté until done. About 10 minutes each side.

Shore Lunch Barbecued Crappie

1 large onion	Salt and pepper
1 bottle Barbecue sauce	Tin foil

Place each fish in a piece of foil. Salt and pepper fish. Place one slice of onion and pour barbecue sauce to cover each fish. Wrap securely. Place in hot coals 12 to 15 minutes.

Freezing Crappie

Frozen fish tend to dry out and absorb some weird flavors if not packaged properly. By freezing fish such as crappie in water, the original flavor is retained, and they are preserved twice as long as would be their normal storage life. They should be completely submerged in water in a container such as a milk carton. Whole crappie can be frozen in ice cream pails, again covered with water.

All fish should be kept frozen at 0 degrees F. and, if possible, it would be even better at –10 degrees F.

The rule of thumb for storage time on fish species is:
Northern Pike/Lake Trout .... 6 months
Bass/Crappie .... 9 months
Walleye .... 10 months

If you are lucky enough to catch fish today but want to hold them overnight before serving them, you might follow these directions for better tasting fillets. If the whole fish is being used and the body has been scaled, marinating time should be increased to one hour. If the crappie are in the pound-plus category, increase marinating time to one hour and thirty minutes.

Wrap them in freezer paper and place in a bowl than can be tightly covered. Store them in the refrigerator.

Keep in mind fresh fish will absorb foul odors rapidly if left unwrapped in a refrigerator, even if just overnight.

It should also be noted fish fillets will keep better if not washed in clean water immediately after filleting. Simply wipe them gently with paper towels, being careful not to handle the fish any more than necessary.

Shore lunch with fried crappie fillets and hot coffee can't be beat.

Odds and Ends for Crappie Cooking:

Having grown up in northern Ontario where fish shore lunches were an every day occurrence during the summer months, I came to prefer my fish fillets plain. Oh, a few drops of lemon or lime juice might be tolerated, but for the most part, a bit of plain flour batter and some hot white Crisco grease was all that was needed to provide a good shore lunch.

But, times change, and as I grew older, with that age came a need to try other things and other ways. And . . . a change in pace, I found out, wasn't all that bad. There are three tasty sauces that can be kept in the refrigerator that truly help a good meal of crappie meat.

Crappie Tartar Sauce

1 cup of mayonnaise   1 tablespoon sweet relish
1 tablespoon minced onions or chives

Combine all ingredients, mix well and you have tartar sauce.

Lemon Butter

4 tablespoons butter	1 tablespoon minced parsley
1 tablespoon lemon juice	2 or 3 drops Tabasco sauce

Melt the butter and add the rest. Lemon butter can be brushed on the crappie fillets while charcoal broiling them on a outdoor grill. This mixture also may be brushed on hot fillets immediately after they are removed from the frying pan.

Mustard Sauce

1 cup of mayonnaise (thin with light cream to suit your needs)
1 teaspoon dry mustard (2 depending on your taste)

Mix together and serve for dip or spread.

There are times when you may wish to bake a crappie whole. Here is a recipe you may find adds variety.

Baked Crappie Stuffing

2 onions, chopped finely	½ pint oysters w/liquid
¼ cup celery, minced	½ cup parsley chopped
¼ cup green pepper, minced	Salt and pepper to taste
1½ cups semi-dried bread crumbs	Thyme (optional)

Saute onions, celery, and peppers in butter until they are softened. Add the oysters and juice and continue cooking for about three minutes. Season to taste, add parsley and bread crumbs and a little thyme if you wish. Pack each fish with stuffing so the stomach cavity bulges slightly. Pin shut if you wish. However, stuffing will brown and hold within the stomach cavity if left unpinned.

Crappie Casserole

1 lb. crappie fillets	1 Tbsp. chopped pimento
3 Tbsp. butter	1 cup grated cheese (¼ lb.)
3 Tbsp. flour	Salt and pepper to taste
1 cup peas	1/3 cup fine dry bread crumbs
2 cups milk	2 Tbsp. melted butter

Leave crappie in large pieces. Soak in cold water for four hours, changing water every hour. Drain and dice the fish. Melt butter. Blend in flour. Slowly stir in milk. Stir constantly over direct heat until thickened. Add grated cheese and seasonings. Fold in peas, pimento, and crappie and turn into a four-cup buttered casserole dish. Stir crumbs into melted butter and sprinkle over top. Bake at 325 degrees for 50 minutes to an hour. Fish should flake easily when done.

There you have it . . . recipes I use often to cook Ol' Silversides. Keep in mind that when properly prepared, crappie meat is delicious!

One of my favorite ways is to have a shore lunch cooked at midday right on the bank.

To cook a successful shore lunch, there are just a few ingredients. You need fillets of crappie . . . of course!

Crisco shortening is best to fry fish over an open fire. Salt and pepper, flour (plain white flour) can be used as a batter.

Three onions to be cut up and placed later in the beans and fried potatoes. One can of pork and beans, one medium-sized can of sliced mushrooms. One large potato for each member of your party. Onions and mushrooms will be added to the potatoes as they fry.

A pair of cast iron frying pans. One pot in which to heat the beans and the additional minced onions and mushrooms.

Charcoal lighter fluid to get damp wood started.

Plates and utensils for each member in your party.

Fix the fire between a pair of green logs. These logs can be used to contain the fire and set the cooking pans on over the fire.

Once the fish are scaled and baked, this platter is ready for the table.

Your bean mix can be placed to one side, at log's end, as you cook the other ingredients of your meal.

Start with the potatoes in frying pan #1. Once these are well on their way to being browned, add the mushrooms and onions. Also, the fish-frying pan and Crisco should now be heating.

Once the shortening is hot, fish fillets can be put in to fry. Fish fillets are the last thing you cook.

Do not overcook crappie fillets. They need but a minute or so on each side if your grease is of proper heat.

Using this formula, a shore lunch can be cooked in less than fifteen minutes. Generally it takes more time to fillet the fish than it does to cook the meal.

No matter where you fish, the cooking of a noon shore lunch will enhance your fishing experience. So . . . I hope you try it. Fish eaten moments after they are caught are the best fish there are.

Dan Gapen readies fish fillets and fried potatoes. Note the gloved hand . . . this precaution saves a lot of burned fingers.

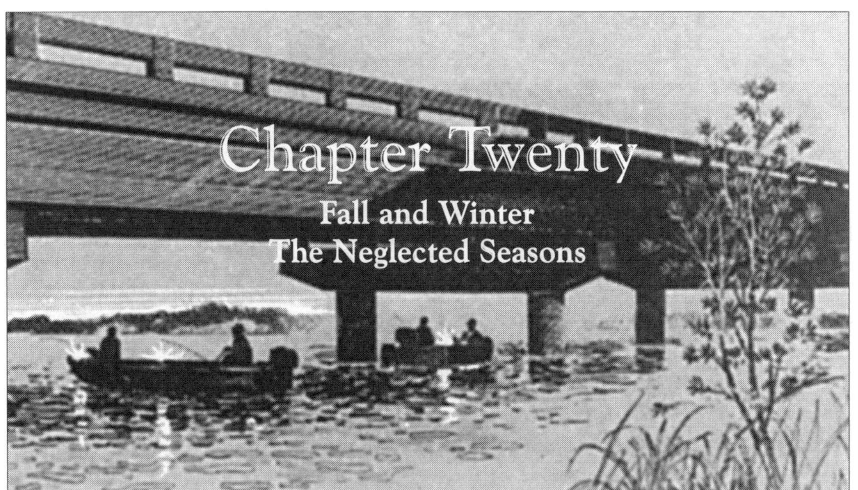

Summer vacation is over. The kids are back in school. Squirrels are gathering acorns and butternuts, and nature's artistic hand has swathed the woods in varied hues of yellow and red. The morning air is crisp, invigorating. It is a great time to be alive, to be outdoors in a duck blind or walking a meandering woodland trail for grouse or squirrel.

Fishing? "Heck, everybody knows that fishing is lousy in the fall and winter!"

Though fall and winter are not noted for the weighty stringers and furious action of spring, they can be surprisingly more productive than many believe. This is especially true with crappie.

During the summer, large schools of crappie drift lazily in the sun-warmed water at varying depths as they seek out cool, shaded and well-oxygenated water. Now as the water begins to cool, the fish become more robust, moving longer distances to find suitable cover and feeding more voraciously than before. Crappie will remain at this level of activity not only through fall, but through the winter months as well.

Fall is especially challenging to the crappie angler. Fish that are found in eight feet of water one day may move to a twenty-foot depth the next. They may be hovering over a brush pile in the morning and move into a deep weed bed by early evening.

Generally, the successful fall anglers fish during mornings and late afternoons. Beginning in September, crappie feed primarily during these two periods, a habit they will maintain on through the winter months.

Photographs provided by *Outdoor Oklahoma Magazine* prove that crappie fishing is for kids of all ages. Fishing docks throughout the southern reservoirs have indeed made crappie angling a sport for all seasons.

Fishing in autumn may necessitate any number of different angling techniques. The deep water jigs mentioned in previous chapters may still

When crappie fishing, a helpful tool is a landing net.

come into play, but most crappie anglers turn to casting small bobber and jig-minnow combinations, or working fly rods in waters from six to fifteen feet.

With cooler temperatures, crappies resume their persnickety eating habits. They will consume more than they did during the hot days of summer, but they take their sweet time at it. Accordingly, the angler should turn to smaller minnows, worms, or nightcrawlers. Crappie are also fond of white grubs and will rise more readily to surface flies.

To overcome the nibbling tactics of finicky fish switch to small bobbers or quill corks. The small size reacts to the slightest disturbance.

A typical fall day would begin with the crappie angler targeting shallow weed beds in protected coves or bays. As the day progresses, move to deeper weed beds, sunken tree tops and submerged brush piles. Toward evening return to shallow, weedy areas where crappie may be preying on minnows and other aquatic organisms seeking refuge in the weeds.

Structure fishing is just as important in fall and winter as the other seasons. A case in point is the long Highway 21 Bridge connect-

Deep-water, log-hugging crappie are fooled by an ugly bug (above). At right: Late evening catch off a willow tree structure.

ing Texas and Louisiana at Toledo Bend Reservoir. Here, anglers tie up to the bridge supports and fish from sunset to midnight.

Often the "Bend" resembles a small city with hundreds of lighted boats dotting the surface. Double-mantled gasoline lanterns are used to attract insects which fall into the water and attract small bait fish. These, in turn, attract the larger predators, including crappie.

Certainly, few anglers brace the cold gusty days of winter. But don't despair, crappie anglers, because a new innovation on many southern reservoirs is providing both comfort and fishing fun for thousands.

Years ago, heated fishing docks or marinas became popular across much of Oklahoma and Texas as well as several other southern states. They were appealing to anglers, offering fishing day or night, all year long, no matter what the weather.

Few people used to weather the winter months in Oklahoma except a few diehards who braved iced lines and freezing feet to string up a mess of crappie.

One cold morning in 1950, a resort operator by the name of Al Radcliff called bait farm owner Sam Williams on Cowskin Arm of Grand Lake in northeast Oklahoma. Al had a friend who owned a cruiser shed (floating dock) across the cove from his resort, at a place then known as Cowskin Lodge, and the crappie were around the shed in droves.

Sam and Al caught all they wanted in less than two hours. It was sleeting, but the enclosed shed was as warm as toast. An idea dawned and Sam wasn't long in putting it into operation. He contacted the owner of the cruiser shed and worked up an agreement whereby he could send his bait customers to that location.

The idea caught on, and people began to jam the shed. As many as 50,000 crappie were taken out of that small cove in ten days.

Sam convinced a friend that the fish dock idea would work on a larger scale, and together they financed "Fish Haven," the nation's first heated dock built expressly for fishing inland waters.

Docks such as these soon floated on several Oklahoma lakes, cabled, anchored and bridged to shore.

Indeed, fishing docks throughout the south have given the crappie angler three to four extra months of fishing fun and comfort. Some were air-conditioned and carpeted and had a TV. But certainly the best attribute was that anglers could nearly always catch crappie.

Marina operators baited their fishing wells with cottonseed cake, fermented grain, hay, sour mash or a combination of these ingredients to attract fish. Brush piles were also strategically located to maintain quality angling.

Unfortunately, most heated fishing docks were limited to about forty to fifty anglers. Though fishing success wasn't guaranteed, the marinas provided many hours of fishing enjoyment at relatively little expense.

An Oklahoma official was known to say: "The nice thing about dock fishin' is that even if the crappie aren't hitting, the conversation, jokes, and friendly atmosphere sure beats sitting at home on a Saturday watching it snow."

Debra Gapen.

Chapter Twenty-One
The Must-Have Panfish Lure

I've been creating new lures and fishing techniques for nearly sixty-five years. Up until now, I haven't developed one as effective as this one on all fish species. The Flicker-Baiter is deadly on all panfish, as deadly as any I've ever created. So deadly that I'm telling you it will likely out-fish any crappie, bluegill, rock bass or perch lure you have in your tackle box.

But, before going on with details, I must tell you the rest of the story.

The Gapen Company has a policy of field testing each new lure that is designed for no less than one year. This includes most effective colors and sizes. The Flicker-Baiter began its tests during 2008, which included both summer and winter tests, before programming it for market.

Too late! A Scandinavian-owned company in Europe brought a similar lure to the United States market during our test time. Without either of us knowing what the other had in mind Gapen's was beat to the punch.

What to do?

The European company's new lure lacked several features Gapen's had implanted into its new creation. The import lacked on ability to represent natural food design or action. Still because of several other features, the import did a good job of catching fish.

Back to the drawing board!

A decision had to be made. Should Gapen's go ahead with distribution of their new creation or cancel the project?

After a year in which the new Flicker-Baiter had sizes and colors added and future field tests done, Dan Gapen, Sr., made the decision in early 2010 to go ahead with the project.

Reasons were simple. Not only did the Flicker-Baiter have its competitors beat in looks and action, but with larger sizes now programmed into the new lure, larger gamefish could be targeted by the new bait.

A lesson learned!

One never knows who or what is happening in lure design and testing in this increasingly smaller fishing industry we compete in.

Do I suggest you buy one of Gapen's new Flicker-Baiters?

Yes, buy several in your favorite fish colors and sizes. I guarantee you'll not be disappointed!

Let me explain further. How and why certain lures are designed.

First: you must make it represent food the species you are trying to attract feed upon.

Second: Your design must effectively attract the fish. This can be done by body design, one which vibrates or wiggles in an enticing natural manner.

Third: An attracting flash or reflection must be part of your lure's design appeal.

Fourth: Your creation must have the proper weight to work its way into the staging structure your fish is found.

Fifth: Smell or scent must be part of your lure's attraction.

Sixth: Sound must be signaled from your lure as its worked, either because of lure design or by mechanics built into your creation.

Seventh: To better enhance the attraction of your lure, live bait or dead bait must be a part of the bait.

Eighth: If natural or live bait is to be part of the lure, it must be placed on the lure in such a way so that an attacking fish easily gains access to it.

Ninth: If natural or live bait is available on your lure, any and all add-ons like this must be able to be used on it.

Tenth: Your creation must attract and catch the species you recommend it for. This should be done throughout all the seasons. This means it must work in open water and through the ice.

At the time I stumbled on the creation of the Flicker-Baiter the lure's main body was already on the market. Gapen's Flicker, a jigging spoon was well on its way to success on a variety of fish species. It had become the company's number one ice lure and was well on its way to success on a variety of other fish species during open water fishing. The Flicker, with its bright red treble hook, in small one-thirty-second- and one-sixteenth-ounce sizes had become top bait to entice panfish during winter months. The larger one-eighth- and one-quarter-ounce sizes worked well as a slab spoon for the summer market when worked on walleye, bass, northern pike, and white bass. The one- and two-ounce sizes were forging their way into the deep water lake trout and striper markets as well as the fork-tailed fish in the saltwater market.

Though the Flicker was working extremely well, there wasn't a really good way to add the final element to it. Live bait and dead bait could be attached to the treble hook, but when tested, the fish we sought often rejected that when they failed to be aggressive enough.

Then one day an idea took hold!

During the previous winter "Bobber" Anne and I had the pleasure of fishing Lake Michigan whitefish with our host Dale Stroschein, owner of Sand Bay Beach Resort in Sturgeon Bay, Wisconsin. Dale had a trick of tying a small #12 treble to the line twelve inches above his main whitefish jig, one of our one-thirty-two-ounce gold Flickers. To the treble, Dale would hook a Berkley one-eighth-inch grub, one they produce to take the place of a maggot or wax worm. Watching how well it worked began to give me an idea. Why not attach a drop line with a hook on it below the Flicker instead of the red treble?

Why below the Flicker? When ice fishing for those whitefish and on outings for perch and other panfish I noticed that, when my Flicker struck bottom, it often forced up a puff of dust. It was to this puff of dust all these panfish first darted. Finding nothing there, they swam upwards and struck the trailing treble hook. What if, when they got down to the puff of dust there was bait waiting for them. In all cases, whitefish, bluegill, and perch were suckers for maggots or mealworms. That gave me the idea to suspend a small hook on mono or wire a couple inches below my Flicker.

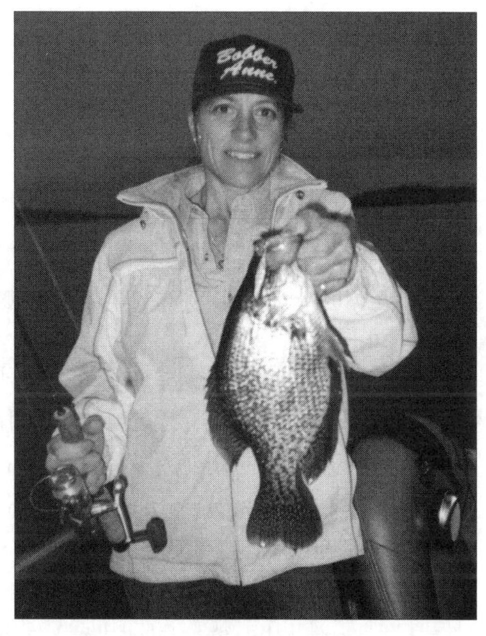

Did it work? Yes! Better than any other panfish enticer I'd ever used. So began the road to testing our new lure, the Flicker-Baiter. To the quarter-ounce size and bigger we place a spread wire dropback line with a hook appropriate to the size of the fish sought. To these hooks we hooked minnows of varying sizes and species depending on the fish we were after. The results were fantastic.

But this is a book on panfish, and I must keep my comments to the Flicker-Baiter to the colors and sizes for these species.

Gapen's manufactures the Flicker-Baiter in only six colors—shad, perch, glow chartreuse, glow firetiger, gold, and silver. The size we suggest for panfish is one-thirty-second and one-sixteenth ounce.

During our testing, we tipped the new lure with maggots, red ball eggs, spikes, wax worms, and of course Berkely's Powerbait. Each worked in varying degrees.

Normally I wouldn't suggest you call Gapen's and ask for a free how-to catalog. But I have so much confidence in the Flicker-Baiter, I'll make the offer. Call the company's toll free number and order at (877) 623-2099.

Chapter Twenty-Two
Crappie on Ice

One of the great mysteries in the world of angling is what motivates the North Country's freeze-up fraternity—that convivial, gregarious bunch of ice fishing enthusiasts who brave blustery winter winds and sub-zero temperatures to pursue their finned quarry.

Ask any angler what lures him onto the frozen expanses of northern lakes and rivers, and he will probably mutter through an icicled moustache, "To catch fish." But it's more than that. There is something stronger that moves people to face such adversity just to catch a few fish.

Of course, the warm-weather fisherman claims he has the answer. He'll argue that his cold weather counterparts lack the common sense to stay out of the cold. But ice fishing has a definite appeal, and ice anglers are definitely hard souls.

In reality, the ice angler may represent the elite of the angling world. He or she is resourceful, cleverly innovative and doggedly persistent in the face of considerable odds.

These men, women, and children with antifreeze in their veins live all over throughout our nation's Snowbelt. Their transitory homes, called ice shanties, reflect true ingenuity. Some are simple in design. But countless other shacks are replete with everything from television sets, built-in bars, battery-powered stereos, self-contained heaters, and yes, even carpeted floors.

Throughout the Cold Belt, these affable snowmen spend countless hours staring into the world of the crappie, sunfish, walleye, pike and perch.

In Minnesota and Wisconsin alone, more than 600,000 anglers pursue the sport of ice angling. And the number-one target of a ma-

Ice fishing's popularily is shown by dense cluster of ice shacks on Minnesota's Lake Minnetonka and in the smile of a young crappie fisherman.

jority of these anglers is the crappie. Why? Because the crappie is easy to catch and requires less angling equipment than any other fish.

The biggest attraction of ice fishing for crappie is its simplicity. It's just a matter of cutting a hole in the ice, baiting a small hook or ice jig with a two-inch minnow, and you're ready for action.

Anyone can catch crappie through the ice, but to add to your angling success and comfort, its best to follow some basic guidelines.

Probably the most important part of ice fishing is your own personal comfort. Nothing ruins an ice fishing trip faster than numb hands or feet. Proper clothing means the difference between enjoying or enduring this sport.

Hands and feet are the most susceptible to cold and thus deserve special attention. Boots should be insulated and waterproof. Felt-lined snow boots are the warmest type of footwear, and chopper-type mittens or snowmobile gloves are effective hand warmers.

Proper clothing consists of lightweight thermal underwear, warm pants and shirt and sweater. Over all this is worn a parka or a snowmobile suit. By wearing several layers of clothes, warm air is trapped between the layers keeping you snug and comfortable. Of course, if you become too warm, it is simply a matter of discarding a garment or two. Excellent outdoor gear is also made by clothing companies designed just for this activity.

Frigid temperatures can also be overcome by wearing electric socks and a knitted facemask. The angler without a fish house can use a small heater to keep warm. Another simple technique is to fill a large coffee can with charcoal briquettes and place it at the edge of the hole. The impromptu heater serves two purposes—it keeps ice from forming on the hole and it is an excellent hand warmer.

Of course the best protection from cold temperatures is the ice house. The angler with a permanent ice shack sometime has an ace in the hole. His "ace" may be a brush pile which he has either placed there or happened upon accidentally. As in summer, crappies gather around brush piles, where they find abundant food and shelter.

To locate these underwater structures, ice anglers will often use a depth finder or any electronic sonar equipment. Once found, the ice shack is placed directly over the brush pile and many a limit of crappie will be plucked from the frigid waters.

Generally the most successful crappie anglers, however, are those with portable houses. These are lightweight, collapsible and can be moved to a new location in a matter of minutes. These anglers know that when action slows, crappie often can be found by cutting another hole, sometimes just a short distance away.

It is very important to remember that the ice angler who moves around, cuts new holes and changes the depth of his bait will usually be the first to discover fishing action.

As mentioned earlier, ice fishing for crappie requires only basic equipment. Crappie and sunfish anglers prefer a short, flexible fiberglass rod with a fixed reel for storing monofilament line. Crappie anglers should not use a line stronger than six-pound test and preferably two or four pounds. Using too heavy a line is a frequent mistake of unsuccessful angling.

Most anglers use small bobbers and small bait. Crappies are finicky feeders in winter. Often they will nip at your bait with the bobber giving no hint to what is happening in the depths below. This problem can be overcome by thinking small.

Use small bobbers, usually no larger than a bottle cap in diameter. Your bait should also be diminutive—a two-inch minnow, or any number

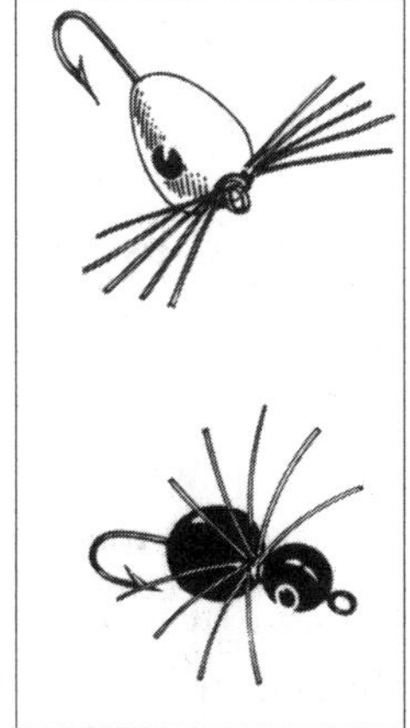

Ice ants.

of grubs, which are the larvae stage of various insects. These include wax worms, golden grubs, mouseys, and others.

A good device when fish are biting light is the almost-submerged bobber. It, too, is more sensitive than conventional floats.

An active minnow is a necessary ingredient, but the ice angler should not be reluctant to give the minnow a helping hand by jigging. This is accomplished by twitching the rod tip every few seconds with about two or three twitches in rapid succession as you slowly raise the rod tip. By raising and lowering the bait, crappie often are enticed into striking.

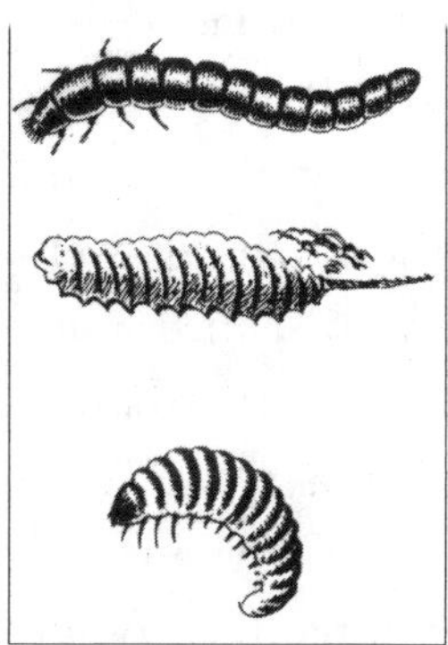

The favorite worms of the ice angler are (from top): golden grub, mousie, and the wax worm.

Crappies show a distinct feeding preference for certain times of the day. This is especially true during winter. Apparently, they just don't like snacking between meals.

Probably the best period is two to three hours after sunrise. Another common time is late in the day, extending until midnight. Many a winter crappie angler swears by night fishing only. They will arrive at their ice shanty after dinner and fish until 11:00 p.m., or even later, with great success.

On days when crappie hit slowly during the early morning hours, I have often witnessed an active feeding period usually starting about eleven in the morning and continuing until an hour or two after noon.

Now that we have some idea of how and when to catch crappie let's try to discover where they lurk under the ice. The angler visiting a lake for the first time sees nothing but a barren, snow-swept wasteland that tells him nothing about the world below the ice.

The best way to find crappie concentrations is to look for angler concentrations. Crappie country is wherever there are clusters of shacks, or anglers fishing next to their cars and campers. And the nice thing about ice anglers is their cheerfulness and genuine willingness to share nature's finned bounty. Walk over and inquire as to their success, how deep they are fishing, and what crappies are biting on. Nine times out of ten the response will be both helpful and cordial.

If there are few anglers on the lake or if they are widely scattered, you may have to find your own school of crappie. In winter, they are usually in relatively deep water—from twenty to as much as fifty feet. Try first in the middle of large, sheltered bays, off rocky points, or about fifty to one hundred yards straight off weed beds. The water depth, of course, will determine the distance you fish from shore.

Oxygen is often at a premium in lakes during winter. Thus fish will tend to congregate in areas where oxygen is entering a body of water, such as inlets of creeks and streams.

Once a likely spot is found, the angler can use either an ice chisel or auger. After the hole is cut, determine the depth by dropping a large sinker to the bottom. Then rig your bait so it will rest from one to two feet off the bottom. If no strikes result, continue to vary the depth at which you fish. Try one depth for several minutes and move your bait farther toward the surface. Crappies are usually caught near the bottom, but you can never be sure at what level they have schooled. I have caught crappies just two feet below the ice in thirty feet of water!

If after trying several depths, the fish still refuse to strike, move on to another spot. Remember, the successful crappie angler is nomadic in the pursuit of fish.

Today, entire families head to ice-covered lakes to their home-away-from-home—that cozy ice shack where the smell of freshly-brewed coffee and the sounds of sizzling hamburgers and warm conversation renew the bonds of love each family shares.

The Old Man and Bobber Anne with some respectable northern black crappie.

Chapter Twenty-Three

All Season Panfishing Summer and Winter

Mille Lacs Lake in central Minnesota, known for its heavy population of walleye, contains a second fish resource few anglers search after. The rock bass and perch populations are immense. Unlike the treasured walleye the other two are generally discarded as by-catch.

I've heard numerous walleye anglers make the claim that the discarded panfish are full of worms making them worthless to the better eating walleye.

Not so! I've found that rock bass and perch don't contain worms in this cold water lake. Only when subjected to warm water do these species carry body worms or maggots, if you will. As a matter of fact some of the best eating fish collected for my winter food have been fillets from the oversized Mille Lacs Lake panfish.

I've spent many an hour each fall fishing this lake to collect fish for my freezer. In both cases, the fillets consist of white meat and, in general, can be larger and thicker than some of the walleye taken from these waters. Many a perch and rock bass reach the two-pound mark on the underwater rock piles Mille Lacs is noted for.

Catching them is easy! All the angler needs is an electric fish finder, a spinning rod with eight-pound line and a one-eighth-ounce

crawfish-colored Ugly Bug jig. Add to this a dozen or so nightcrawlers for tipping, and you're set.

Why the crawlers and Ugly Bugs? Both species feed heavily on crawfish year round. Tipping this jig, which resembles their favorite food, adds the proper scent.

Presentation is likewise easy. Station your boat directly over the fish found on the locator and vertically present your bait down to them. Normally, both species will stage within a foot of the rocky bottom. Once your Ugly Bug touches bottom, lift slightly and work the lure in short, tantalizing lifts. Both fish are known as fast strikers. You'll know immediately when the bite occurs.

The same rock pile, this time moving along their bottom edges instead of the upper structure, will give up these species in winter.

One small tip: During hot summer months rock bass are easily attracted by the use of leeches. The leech is a favorite food during August.

When rock isn't available in the water you fish, work downed tree trunks and water-inundated tree stumps. It's here that you'll find large schools of rock bass seeking shelter. Wood and rock are structures

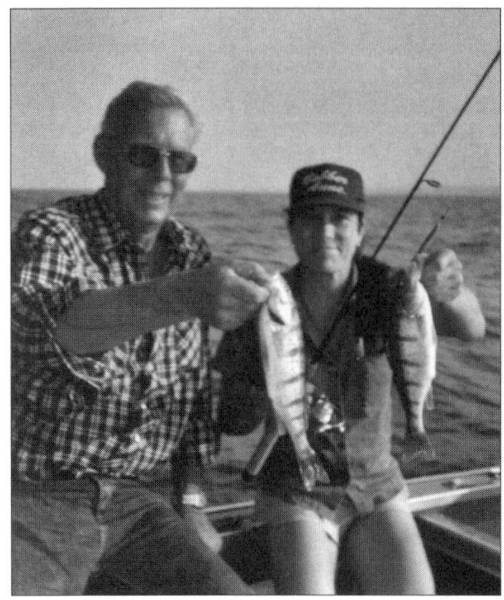

this fish reproduces on. They dig rock spawning beds, similar to those of a bluegill, on rocky structures in the gravel between boulders or on wood, generally beneath a waterlogged tree trunk.

Now, let me tell you a story about the perch.

Too many years ago when teenage bravado pushed this author to pursue the unknown, I discovered the perch. It occurred on giant Lake Superior at a place called Pays Plat Point along the great lake's northern shore near the town of Nipigon in the Province of Ontario.

Six of us, four tourists from Iowa, myself, and Dan Bushard, a native guide, while working for my father's resort Chalet Bungalow Lodge on the Nipigon River, were searching for walleye or large northern pike. Unknown to any of us, perch had selected the rocky weed-covered point to spawn on. This phenomenon had probably occurred for endless years before our arrival.

Casting Dardevle spoons, red and white in color, we'd successfully engaged a number of large pike when one of my guests set hook into a darkly striped walleye type fish. It was the first perch caught by any of us on Nipigon Bay. Amazingly, the fish was nearly two pounds and presented a beautiful trophy. She had come out of six feet of clear water on the rocky point. It was June and obviously the perch spawn was on. The fish was kept for later identification.

During the next hour while working the structure for pike, I noticed several places where similar striped fish would dart and cross the stony flat as we passed over the point. The guest from Iowa expounded great admiration for the striped fish he'd brought to the boat. That

lasted only a couple min-
utes as a large twenty-pound
pike was engaged on his second cast after boating the
perch.

Back at the resort Dad
explained to me that the
fish was called a perch, and
was a favorite food fish of
both pike and walleye. And,
that perch this size were
highly prized in the States

as an excellent eating species. I filleted the two-pounder and it was
served to the angler from Iowa that evening for dinner. He raised so
much of a ruckus about how good it was that another trip to search
out the Pays Point perch was planned. My question had to be answered
by my dad and my Iowa guest. I was told perch loved worms and that
a bobber, a hook, and sinker were the best way to catch them. Of
course, I had no bobbers, but this problem was remedied by a search
of my guest's tackle box. In it were several red-and-white pointed cork
floats. When asked if the color had any enticement to catch this fish,
I received a blank look and an uncertain answer.

That night I gathered three or four dozen nightcrawlers, the clos-
est thing to garden worms we had available. Tomorrow would produce
a new adventure in fishing!

To get to the Lake Superior point we had to travel twenty-four
miles by the Lodge's cruiser, the *Dan-Vau-Don*. Behind this twenty-
eight-footer we towed two eighteen-foot canvas and wood freighter canoes. These would be our fishing platforms.

I'd been instructed to bring home as many of the striped beauties
as we could catch. At that time perch weren't even a game fish and
there was no limit on them. We'd treat all forty-two guests at our resort
with a meal of fresh perch fillets the next night.

With the cruiser anchored, our canoes departed toward the rocky point and the site of fleeting striped fish below. It took but minutes to find the first group, all clustered around a series of large boulders. My lesson began as my guest showed me how to use the bobber fishing technique. At this point in my life I'd never seen a bobber presentation.

No sooner had the one-and-one-half-inch round bobber hit the water and its worm cargo settled than it was "Bobber down!" I can't tell you that fishing one- to two-pound perch on a metal casting rod loaded with black twenty-five-pound line was what I called sporting but it certainly was exciting to watch the float disappear.

I'll not bore you with the details but by the end of our day we'd gathered 117 fat Lake Superior perch, enough to feed all out guests and the staff as well. I'd have to fillet them all, as I did the weekly catch of dinner walleye on Friday night. Like the walleye, the perch filleted easily.

That evening my mother and waitress Della proudly walked into the main dining room announcing "perch" would be the special treat for our guests that night. Results came after dinner as guest after guest congratulated Mom on how delicious the evening meal had been. Many of them had never eaten perch. The boys from Iowa became camp heroes that week.

Since then I've fished the striped fish wherever I can, and found them to be a special challenge during winter when bait presentation is done under the ice.

During my winter outings I've gained a great knowledge of the perch habits in many of our water structures. Observation via an underwater camera such as a Marcum has shown me that winter perch are always on the move. They come and go beneath ice holes in schools. Traveling territory may only cover a hundred foot circle or as little as twenty feet in either direction. In some lakes, this moving mass of schooled perch will travel as far as a half mile in travel distance.

One thing you can count on is that, if perch were there when you began, they'll be back. So, my advice is to sit tight, continue to observe and continue to fish.

Winter perch bait will vary slightly from summer offering. Though worms were the number one attractor in summer, small minnows and wax worms work better under the ice. Small metal ice jigs such as a Waxy, Teardrop, or Hog-n-Jig loaded with this natural bait will do the trick. If you are looking for a special lure to entice winter perch, choose a Flicker or a Flicker-Baiter in one-sixteenth ounce loaded with a red ball egg.

Because winter waters appear clearer due to the lack of surface wave action, your line test may need to be reduced from eight to four pound test.

The key to winter perch fishing success is that tip I gave you previously. Remember, winter perch are a nervous traveler. There's no need for you to take on a similar pattern. Sit tight!

Now, I'd like to end my book on panfish with a very special species near and dear to my heart. It isn't a panfish, but instead a member of the salmon family. The common lake whitefish isn't considered a gamefish in angling circles. Instead its called an uncatchable commercial species not worthy of gamefish status.

To the angler, such remarks are insulting to the whitefish's character. Most of the gamefish pros will tell you a whitefish can't be caught on a hook and line. Once again, Not So! This writer has been catching whitefish on rod and reel since the age of twelve. At my parents' fishing resort a huge migration of whitefish ascended the Nipigon River to feed on the annual hatch of mayflies on Lake Helen, a widening of the Nipigon.

In those days we approached this fish with dry flies that floated on the water's surface. Angling was done with a fly rod, generally a four-five weight, a fly reel loaded with fly line and fifty yards of Dacron black line backing, a seven foot clear gut leader and a #12 brown bivisible dry fly. To better attract the whitefish feeding on the mayflies on surface, we'd place our fly in an area where few natural flies existed. Whitefish seem better adapted at targeting a single fly set apart by itself than one in the midst of a heavily grouped population of natural flies.

Whitefish are found across Canada and throughout the northern United States. They mainly populate lakes but will forge their way into rivers if the insect life they feed on is available. Being a school fish, the whitefish feeding during summer will be seen cruising the shallow waters of your favorite walleye lake as they porpoise in and out of the surface sucking in the recently hatched insect life. The shad fly, or mayfly hatch generally brings the most activity.

Knowledgeable anglers know that a traveling school of whitefish that passes by will soon return along the same path. Generally, in a lake this migration path will encompass a quarter to a half mile long trek.

For more information on the whitefish, pick up a copy of my most recent hardback book, *Adventure Fishing the Americas* at www.gapen.com or by calling Toll-FREE (877) 623-2099.

Though known to be a very difficult species to catch during summer days, the whitefish can also be taken through the ice in winter. Examples of this are seen on Lake Simcoe, Nipigon, and Georgian Bay in Ontario. Another key area to target winter whitefish is Sturgeon Bay in Lake Michigan. Here, guide services such as my friend Dale Stroschein of Sand Bay Beach Resort at Sturgeon Lake, Wisconsin, provide warm winter ice houses over deep water where whitefish are readily taken. "Bobber" Anne and I experienced such an outing the winter before this book was published.

Dale, an accomplished angler and guide had invited us to give a try at winter ice fishing for whitefish after he heard I loved to angle the species. We would arrive the first week of January to start the adventure. There'd be a television show recorded during the three days we fished. This meant we'd have to use underwater cameras to record the action below the ice. One camera was put on the bottom where the whitefish roamed during these cold days and one ten feet under the house to record the fighting action. This would enable me to learn more about the species, its habitat and feeding practices.

With the house heater on and ice holes opened up, it was time to fish. Bob Kook, our camera man gave the word and we all dropped our Flickers into the fifty-two feet of water. Below, a ten-foot-wide ridge was readily visible beneath us. On either side, depth plunged off into dark water 100 feet or more.

Schools of lake whitefish came to this underwater ridge each day to nose out aquatic insect larvae and tiny minnows which had taken shelter in the patches of sand between the rough rock on the ridge. Dale explained, "To be successful, we need to get our bait down on these sand patches, bounce them up and down and create a small cloud of disturbed sand dust." It's a common practice for whitefish to nose into the sand, lift their noses upwards to create these tiny clouds of dust. Such practice dislodges their food so it can be consumed.

Watching through the ice hole in combination with the bottom camera, it was showing us several fish hone in on Dale's Flicker as it bounced off sand bottom. A second after it immerged from its second bounce a whitefish sucked in the red treble hook. We had our first Lake Michigan whitefish. Thumper, my yellow Labrador, excitedly nuzzled the silver fish as it flopped on the ice house floor at Dale's feet. Yes, Anne and I had brought my dog along ice fishing.

It took Anne and me several presentations of our Flickers to catch on to the proper working of our baits. During that time Dale landed two more whitefish.

We did catch on, and on the first day saw the three of us toss twenty-one whitefish on the ice outside the house.

There was another trick Dale showed us. Twelve inches above his Flicker, Dale had suspended a #12 treble hook. On the hook he inserted a small mousey-size piece of Berkley Gulp. Often the whitefish drawn to the puff of sand would key in on this and strike it. This was done whenever the Flicker below was obscured by sand dust for any length of time. In the end, forty percent of his fish came on the suspended treble.

This gave me the idea I described in Chapter 21. The observation of Dale using his trick treble stimulated my idea to create the Flicker-

Baiter. As a matter of fact on our second day with Dale I'd rigged a Flicker with a monofilament trailer to which a #12 treble hook was attached. To this hook, a spike or mousey was intermittently impaled. It worked wonderful! All you had to do in your presentation was to elevate the new lure (Flicker-Baiter) up off the sand pockets far enough to free it from the enveloping cloud of disturbed sand. Instantly, the whitefish honed in on the suspended grub. It was a natural reaction, as if a fly larva had been blown from within the sand patch.

I realize whitefish aren't part of the panfish family but for this fellow, one of my favorites. They can be worked with the same gear, lures and bait that catch all the panfish species. The whitefish has also been considered one of the top food species by man for as many years back as I can remember.

No longer can your fishing buddy look down his nose at the favorite fish of my youth with disdain. Whether the whitefish is caught in summer when they're caught on artificial flies and leap like a tarpon or caught out of fifty feet of water on delicate ice tackle this fish deserves to be called a GAMEFISH.